30 DAYS
to TRANSFORMATION

with

CAROLINA M. BILLINGS, DORTHA HISE, EAN PRICE MURPHY, DR. ELISA MAGILL, GINA DE LEON, KIM WARD, MELANIE HERSCHORN, MINDY MCMANUS, MONIKA GRECZEK, SALLIE WAGNER, SIMONE SLOAN, STACEY HALL, STEPHANEY CAMPBELL, YOUSSEF SKALLI

Produced by

CAROLINA M. BILLINGS

Copyright © 2022 Carolina M. Billings | Powerful Women Today

ALL RIGHTS RESERVED. This book contains material protected under International and Federal Laws and Treaties. Any unauthorized reprint or use of this material is prohibited. No portion of this book may be reproduced, stored in a retrieval system, or transmitted in any form or by any means — electronic, mechanical, photocopy, recording, scanning, or other — without express written permission from the authors or publisher, except for brief quotations in critical reviews or articles. It is illegal to copy this book, post it to a website, or distribute it by any other means without permission from the authors and publisher.

Published by PWT Publishing

A division of Powerful Women Today

3 Centre St. #202, Markham, ON

L3P 3P9 Canada

Publisher: Carolina M. Billings' email: info@powerfulwomentoday.com

Limits of Liability and Disclaimer of Warranty

The author and publisher shall not be liable for the reader's misuse of this material. This book is for strictly informational and educational purposes.

Disclaimer

The views expressed are those of the author and do not reflect the official policy or position of the publisher or Powerful Women Today.

Copyright Use and Public Information

Unless otherwise noted, images have been used according to public information laws.

ISBN:

Paperback ISBN: 978-1-7782536-5-2

EBook ISBN: 978-1-7782536-6-9

CONTENTS

Foreward 5

Publisher's Note 7

Introduction 11

Radical Self Respect 27

Championing Your Own Adventure 51

The 5 Secrets of Trans-Flow-Mation 67

10 Tiny Transformations That Create An Abundantly
Prosperous Life 81

New Baby And Me 97

From "Yes" To "Forever" (The Empowered Couple) 113

Transforming Your Relationship to Money 123

The Energy Transformation Equation 137

Should I Stay Or Should I Go? 155

How To Become A Subject Matter Expert 169

Tapping Into The Power Of Transformation 185

Healthy Habits 199

Transformation: Your Strategy For Life................... 207

Transforming Toxic Rockstars Into Servant Leaders 221

A Transformation Journey Towards Cultural Humility 237

Conclusion 253

Acknowledgements 262

Special Thanks... 263

About Powerful Women Today & PWT Publishing......... 264

Other Books By PWT Publising 272

Foreward

Lucia St. Amour
Best Selling Author For the Forces of Good

We are never done transforming. We continue on a journey but never arrive. How exciting that the curiosity and learning stay alive in us - especially if we feed it; especially if we don't yield to complacency; especially if we don't accept without question the patterns of messaging and behaviour that have insidiously informed our interactions and that may not be serving our whole being.

The everyday superpower of negotiation is a transformative power that too many women, in particular, have not harnessed. Negotiation isn't just for business; it's everybody's business. It's all around us every day from the bedroom to the kitchen, to the grocery store parking lot, to the board room. If you haven't tapped into your everyday negotiating superpowers, there's great news: you have it, you can hone it, and it will transform your everyday life to something where you can confidently show up in every aspect.

May you never finish transforming.

S. Lucia Kanter St. Amour
Attorney | Author | VP of Board UN Women San Francisco

LinkedIn
Podcast
Best-Selling Book

Publisher's Note

Carolina M. Billings

I am beyond thrilled to have the opportunity to expand the Mission and Vision of Powerful Women Today to Champion and Empower Women's Emotional and Financial Independence

As you can see, 30 Days to Transformation is a guide. What our Mentor Experts write about are the product of decades long continuous formal and self-directed learning, documenting, testing, failing, reflecting, and understanding. All this learning has been summarized into 15 inspirational and aspirational chapters.

To say that these 30-Day Challenges and the steps to achieve them will take 30 minutes, 30 weeks or 30 years is to begin to understand that life is organic and on-going. It may as well be 30 lifetimes.

The biggest takeaway from this book is the need to take ACTION. It is knowing that there is only one person who has the ability to direct your life. That person is YOU.

Big Love.

Carolina

Photo Credit: Pheasant Lane Photography

How to make contact:
Publisher@PowerfulWomenToday.com

Love After Love

*The time will come
when, with elation
you will greet yourself arriving
at your own door, in your own mirror
and each will smile at the other's welcome,
and say, sit here. Eat.
You will love again the stranger who was yourself.
Give wine. Give bread. Give back your heart
to itself, to the stranger who has loved you
all your life, whom you ignored
for another, who knows you by heart.
Take down the love letters from the bookshelf,
the photographs, the desperate notes,
peel your own image from the mirror.
Sit. Feast on your life.
Derek Walcott*

"A girl should be two things:
who and what she wants."
- Coco Chanel

INTRODUCTION

TRANSFORMATION

[TRANS-FER-MEY-SHUHN]

NOUN

The act or process of transforming. the state of being transformed. change in form, appearance, nature, or character.
Meriam Webster

HOW YOU DEFINE TRANSFORMATION MATTERS TO YOUR SUCCESS AND HAPPINESS.

Change is inevitable. It is often said that change is the only constant. Sometimes we're prepared for it, other times not. You always hope for the former -- for change to be deliberate, strategic and brought on by the opportunity to transform.

Change however is not the same as transformation. As humans, we experience transformation at many points in our life organically. We Transform from an infant to a toddler, transforming from a woman to a mother, midlife offers transformation by sending our hormones into a dance or a revolution sometimes both at the same time. Eventually organically transform into elders, sages if you will, understanding and remembering a life full of opportunities taken and more often than not missed.

In fact, transformation is essential to longevity. This brings us to the consideration of the empowerment of intentional transformation. Whether brought on by internal discoveries and insights or necessitated by external forces, we ought to consider the impact of not being an active participant in developing the person we choose to be, the experiences we choose to have and purposely minimizing the loss of potentially transformative moments.

To thrive in today's ever-changing world, transformation by choice is imperative. But there are many ways to do it. The one constant is your role, as the author of your own life, and the need for your direct involvement.

Put simply, we can no longer afford to maintain the status quo. We need to be ready to take educated risks; be constantly on the lookout for disruptive patterns, toxic environments and things or people that simply no longer work for us; and be willing to set a transformative, vision that enables us to capitalize on opportunities, counter any threat and maximize value. Transformation when self-determined, can result in the highest level of personal fulfillment.

The question is, how? how do we determine our exact role, the exact time or the modalities to be used in transformation? And where should we focus our finite time and energy to best help you succeed on this journey?

> *If you can't handle me at my worst ... you don't deserve me at my best.*
> *Marilyn Monroe*

TRANSFORMING SELF

Transformation by Radical Self-Respect by Carolina Billings

Radical Self-Respect is about changing our mindsets and changing how we look at our own lives. It is about taking ownership and responsibility for how we treat ourselves and how we let other people treat us. It is understood that if we are constantly being mistreated, we are cooperating with the treatment. I hear many people complain that they would do anything for others, but they rarely get the same treatment in return.

Oddly enough, setting boundaries begins within. Boundaries are about what you choose to let into your life, whom you chose to let into your life and the experiences and life you choose to live. In my experience, there are two philosophies that help not only find inner peace but make the journey a delightful celebration of personal independence: Taoism and Mindfulness Meditation.

Mindfully Empowered
better yet
Mind Fully Empowered

Being Open to Receive by Dortha Hise

Sometimes being open to receiving can appear in ways that you don't anticipate. For example, receiving peace about a situation where there was struggle previously. Or perhaps it comes in allowing yourself permission to receive.

Being gentle with yourself throughout the process is a necessary step in order to allow what will come to show up.

And while it may sound like I'm speaking in riddles or circles about receiving as a magical thing that which will render itself with a beacon and a strobe light somewhere, it's not that. Sometimes the inner things that we work on don't show up in a physical manifestation of a "thing," rather as peace or calmness, or satisfaction, etc.

Sometimes the gift of receiving is in that openness **to** receive it.

The Secrets of Transflowmation by Kim Ward

Mindset and personal growth become a new part of my days. I learned about afformations. Don't confuse this with affirmation. Affirmations are a positive sentence, but what happens when you read or write a sentence that your brain knows is a lie?

Each morning, start your day with one powerful question that only has a positive outcome. Mine was "How can I show up more powerfully today?" This question is called an afformation. It's not a lie and your brain will be determined to find an answer for this question. Before you know it, you will start to behave in a way that solves this question.

It took me a year and a half to build a global, multiple-six-figure business from home. I was Living my dream of time, freedom, financial independence, and impacting so many people, starting in my own home.

TRANSFORMING RELATIONSHIPS

10 Tiny Transformations That Create an Abundantly Prosperous Life by Stacey Hall

During my early adulthood, I was often a negative person, having grown up in a household that focused on what was wrong…instead of what was good in our lives.

I was eventually introduced to the concept that we manifest what we focus upon, and I realized that I could change my outlook through focused effort and attention. I made a pact with myself to create a set of tools and resources – tiny transformations -- that I would use every day to keep my physical, emotional, mental, and spiritual energy as abundantly high as possible. I call these tools and resources my 'Energy Surges' because they boost my attitude up to the highest heights of positivity and prosperity.

It is much easier to be a positive and prosperity-minded person when we feel our decisions are energizing and empowering and support us to take an action from a sense of desire, passion, commitment, and/or intention.

The Transformational Effect of a Little One on Health, Work, and Relationships by Leona Krasner

Baby-making and work. What an adventure. From the get-go, I knew I would go back to work sooner rather than later after baby boy was born. The moment he was out, however, I knew the focus would have to be on him. The key was reprioritizing my life such that baby was front and center.

I am the Founder and Managing Partner of a ten-employee law firm that helps folks in New York and New Jersey with their family law needs. I had two key goals as they related to work and my baby:

1. My baby would be nourished almost fully with my milk; and
2. I wanted to maximize my time with my little love to the greatest degree I could.

People talk about how much of a burden a new baby puts on a relationship. Heck, I see it in my law practice all the time. But surely that wouldn't happen to me.

Turns out that caring for a whole new human, coupled with way less sleep than we had ever had before, meant that the pressure hit us, even though I did not expect it to do so. Communication was key. My husband asking me in those first post-birth days how I was feeling, really, made such a difference. Taking the time over dinner, or whichever five-minute meal we could grab before baby let us know he was up again, to share our worries, best practices, latest internet or Facebook mommy group discoveries we had learned, and plan together, made all the difference.

From Yes to Forever by Stephaney Campbell

Many couples may underestimate the power of marriage preparation. Some couples are even reluctant to the idea as they may feel it to be an outdated practice. As the saying goes "An ounce of prevention is worth a pound of cure".

Whether you're newly engaged, planning your wedding day, or have been married for years, it can come as a shock for couples to experience challenges, disagreements, and struggles in their relationships. All too often, couples approach the big day with the assumption that the marriage of fairy tales will be theirs, that their love will always be enough, and that maintaining their relationship while taking care of themselves as individuals will be easy.

As wonderful as that may sound, all couples face challenges, now challenges. Now we have created a plan to help couples build that foundation. My brilliant mentor, Hailey Party and -founder of the Happy Love marriage preparation workshop, has taught me how to guide couples and help them insulate their marriages using 5 essential steps to creating an IDEAL marriage. This method has helped me in my relationship, as well as in the couples I have coached.

Transforming Relationships with Money by Ean Price Murphy

I had always thought of money as a necessary evil, a unit of exchange in which I begrudgingly gave up my time so that I could pay my bills. When I started working for myself, I could set my price based on what I wanted to charge to have a comfortable life - not just what a boss was able to afford to pay me. When I was able to charge based on the value I provided and find clients who wanted the services I was offering, my relationship to money transformed.

The daily stress and worry dissipated and I found that most months I had a little extra money to do with as I wished. Conversations with myself about my goals and values and how I wanted to save or use the excess became normal. I was able to put money away for retirement, save for vacations, and support charities that were important to me. I came to realize that money is necessary to be able to catalyze the changes I wanted to see in my life, my community, and the world. Now I no longer view money as a unit of exchange for time, but for impact. I no longer view money as neutral but as a tool for good.

TRANSFORMING YOUR WORLD

Harness Your Energy to Transform Your Ideas into Reality by Elisa Magill

> *"Everything is energy & that's all there is to it. Match the frequency of the reality you want and you cannot help but get that reality. It can be no other way. This is not philosophy. This is physics."*
> *~ Darryl Anka*

Today, self-help books are abundant and available to us from multiple sources. Many of these books discuss the potential to create our own realities. Is it "fluff?" Is it something a "con-artist" came up with to steal millions from those who wish it to be true? Some would say this is the case. However, the research shows that there is something to the belief we share in a cause. In a sense, when we think something and believe it to be true, we are energizing that belief. We are giving it life. When we continue to envision that reality, our brain will believe it to be true, and will work to make that belief a reality (Hill, 2008).

This is why some research will show that visualization works. If the brain thinks negatively, it will negatively charge our thoughts, and our negative thoughts and actions will follow. However, if our brain envisions positive outcomes, our thoughts and actions will follow in that desired direction as well. In this way, we can build momentum and energy in any direction we choose.

Should I stay or should I go by Gina Marie De Leon

Often, I see people moving companies and running into the exact same reasons they initially decided to move because they never addressed the underlying issue, which is their lack of belief. Be honest with yourself in this area. Have you given the company a fair try, and focused on all the right things? What specifically needs to change for it to work, and do you have reasonable grounds on which to believe that is likely to happen and in what time frame? Do you believe that another company is more aligned with your vision, are you passionate about it and believe it is a better place for you?

Whether you stay or go, make the decision, and plant your flag, because the people that have made an impact and have become financially successful in this business are those that stood the test of time. It is all right if you want to go somewhere else, but do not be a company hopper the minute things get tough, or you are never going to have staying power in this profession. The people that have staying power are the ones that find a company that they are aligned with in terms of their values, they believe the leadership has character and integrity, they love the products, and it is a fair compensation plan, and they plant their flag in the ground and they get to work, ride the ups and downs, they understand they there are good years in the and bad years, but they never waver. They have a vision, and they keep going, and that is why they succeed.

Let Transformation commence!

"Not all transformations are visible."
Anonymous

Carolina M. Billings

Dedication

To the two forces constantly transforming my life,

my father and my son.

Two fierce men whose love, respect and pride are

and will always be my true north.

Dr. Carlos Munoz Barillas and Charlie Billings

my everything is for you.

CHAPTER 1

RADICAL SELF RESPECT

SETTING OUR BOUNDARIES AND KNOWING OUR NON-NEGOTIABLES

By Carolina M. Billings

Radical Self-Respect is about changing our mindsets and changing how we look at our own lives. It is about taking ownership and responsibility of how we treat ourselves and how we let other people treat us. It is understanding that if we are constantly being mistreated, we are cooperating with the treatment. I hear many people complain that they would do anything for others, but they rarely get the same treatment in return.

Oddly enough, setting boundaries begins within. Boundaries are about what you choose to let into your life, who you chose to let into your life, and the experiences and life you choose to live. In my experience, there are two philosophies that help not only find inner peace, but make the journey a delightful celebration of personal independence: Taoism and Mindfulness.

Mindfully Empowered

better yet

Mind Fully Empowered

Taoism is a philosophy which emphasizes becoming one with the rhythms of nature, which is known as The Way. Lao Tsu is credited as the writer of Taoism's most sacred text the I Ching book of Change, in which he associates the process of achieving real happiness with managing the four fundamental areas of life:

Resources, Relationships, Self-Development, and Self-Maintenance

The old master's teachings, even after two and a half thousand years, are world-renowned, studied and practised by millions around the world.

Reflecting and beginning to know who you are through the four fundamental areas of life, helps to understand not only who you are, but what you want and do not want to have in your life. After all, you are 100% in control of your mind, body, and spirit.

Number One: Resources.

Having your resources at peace is like stretching a bow. The high is lowered, the low is raised, the excess is reduced, and the deficiency is replenished. The Way reduces the excess and replenishes deficiency. People's way is often not so.

What the Tao tries to tell us is that we have to avoid excess and replenish deficiency.

In other words, we need to take care of all of our resources in an equal way. Resources do not only mean money, it can be anything which can be traded or can be anything you use for your daily well-being. This includes money and possessions.

For example, your house, your car, your brain power, your talents, and your physical abilities.

Flow and Balance

In Taoism, there is a concept of Yin and Yang that says that each aspect of nature is dual, and we need to balance the opposites in order to live in harmony with nature.

Yin is passive, and Yang is the active principle of duality; this duality can be seen in all patterns of nature, such as in the annual cycle of winter and summer, the daily cycle of night and day. Yang are complementary parts of Chi, which is the vital force driving us.

If Tao was like an ocean connecting everything, Chi is an energy pattern. It is the wave when our Chi is balanced between Yin and Yang and is flowing smoothly. This leads to a fulfilled life.

The concept of balancing the complementary parts can be applied to the subject of resource management. We have to make sure we don't use too much of one resource at the expense of another.

When you use your talents in your job to excess, you get promoted, and you enjoy doing overtime at work, doing what you love, but you completely ignore your health. You don't take your time to replenish your physical power in the long run. This can be very detrimental, and can even shorten your life. If you use one resource to excess, you end up creating disharmony in the universe.

Your vital force *Chi* will not be balanced, and as a consequence, you can feel tired, irritable, and stressed. You can even feel pain, actual muscle weakness. It can affect your health, and you may underperform in other areas of your life, just like any structure or a building that is supported by equal upright pillars. The resources you have are the pillars of your well-being you have to nurture and balance all of them.

Managing resources in our everyday lives.

Be it in what we eat, what we wear, and how we live, how we work might just be the antidote to our stressful modern consumption-led world, as Taoism Embraces a more balanced approach. That is to say, having just enough to meet your needs, not your wants. This leads to living a sustainable lifestyle that embraces the pleasures of existence rather than those of consumption, and when you focus on the pleasures of existence, you live.

The Way is simple. Be life.

Number two: Relationships

The mindful mind and spirit do not hoard, it does for others. The more it has, the more it gives to others, and the ever more he gets to live. According to Tao, you must live in harmony with everything around you, your community, nature, and with the universe as a whole. How would you like to turn your innate passion for helping other people into a prosperous part?

Living in harmony means to do no harm and, moreover, to nurture, protect, and contribute to the well-being of everything around you. As all humans are part of this universe, we have to see others as our extended family. We have to take care of each other.

In Taoism, there is a cosmic principle which says that everything you do will eventually come back to you in one way or another. Thus, if we care about others, if we give our help and support, these good deeds will come back to us in the end. We will receive back even more care, love, and support.

On the contrary, if we hurt other people and the environment, we are not acting in harmony with human society, and the universe and the harm we did to others will harm us even more in the end. The moral is that everything you do to others or the environment is a seed of everything that will be done to you later.

> *"No person is an island, and being happy has much to do with the relationship between you and what surrounds you."*

Scientific studies prove the importance of having a healthy social life. For example, a Harvard study on adult development found that good relationships are the key factors that matter most for long-lasting happiness. Good relationships keep us happier and healthier. One of the most important ways to achieve lifelong happiness is to focus on meaningful relationships and on trying to improve or eliminate the bad relationships in our lives.

Number three: Self-Development

To quote Lao Tsu, a great nation is like a great man. When he makes a mistake, he realizes it. Having realized it, he admits it. Having admitted it, he corrects it. He considers those who point out his faults as his most benevolent teachers. Striving for excellence should be a primary focus in life.

In Taoism. To achieve excellence means to achieve an advanced level of self-mastery, to stop taking things personally, to think before reacting, to know how to listen to criticism and to learn from it.

Mastering your fears and emotions is the key to achieving happiness.

Taoist masters always talked about the importance of the words you use and the things you do, because they become the house you will live in, which means they have great consequences for your life. They can repair your well-being to live happily. You have to build a beautiful house from your words and actions.

"The words you use, and the things you do, because they become the house you will live in."

Self-mastery plays a major key in people who spend enough time working on self-development and self-mastery to understand themselves in a better way. They can control their thoughts. They know how to avoid negative thinking. And they know how to learn from their mistakes.

"Growing personally leads to more happiness"

The first test of self-mastery is to be able to realize and take responsibility for your mistakes, and then correct them. Oftentimes this can prove to be very difficult. We're blinded by pride and by the fear to lower ourselves in the eyes of others. So, we cover up our mistakes with lame excuses. However, by passing this simple but important test, you can prove to be a mature person capable of recognizing and, indeed, correcting your mistakes.

The second test is to be able to listen to and learn from the people who criticize you and point out your faults. It takes strength and discipline to be able to hide your anger and embarrassment while listening to hard criticism. But this is what you should do if you want to learn from your mistakes and polish your character.

Moreover, mindfulness suggests that you also have to be grateful when somebody points out your mistakes, as it is a great opportunity for you to become aware of your faults and to improve yourself.

To pass these two tests you first need the right mental attitude. You need to understand that your mistakes are not statements about who you truly are, but are indicators of where you are at that moment to go further. You need to know where you are, and what kind of mistakes you're still making, and you need the proper map.

"Your mistakes are not statements about who you truly are, but are indicators of where you are at the moment."

The teachers are the people who point out your defects as a useful practice. Stop for a few minutes every evening and write down the mistakes you made, think about what criticism you received that day, and make a plan to correct the mistakes and character defects that have been pointed out to you.

Follow it, and keep a record of your improvements in Taoism. Discipline is not based on self-motivation, but on mastering your energies. If you're able to master your energies, then you'll have the maturity to correct your mistakes and learn from the criticism you receive.

Number four: Self-Maintenance

We learn from Lao Tsu "He who treasures his body as much as the world can be a treasure for the world." "He who loves his body as much as the world can be entrusted with the world." Self-maintenance in Taoism means respecting your body and respecting yourself.

"How you treat yourself is teaching others how they can treat you"

The human body is said to have its own energy pattern, which is known as Zang Fu. The Zang Fu model has particular organs that correspond to the five elements; wood, fire, earth, metal, and water. The organs have Yin and Yang properties assigned which, if not balanced, will result in particular illnesses to keep the Yin and Yang energies in balance.

Taoism recommends the practice of Wu Wei, which means doing action through non-action. In other words, to be in a flow state to do things effortlessly by practicing, or why we can reach a state of complete spontaneity and happiness.

The state of Zen. Peace within your boundaries.

In Taoism. You're happy when you are able to follow the spontaneous course of things. And so, to achieve a state of happiness, you have to know how to balance the Yin and Yang energies in your body. Sometimes our body has too much Yin, and sometimes too much Yang.

Yin regulates the parasympathetic nervous system, the rest and the digestive state. Yang, the sympathetic nervous system, is the vital flight state which is most typically activated by danger. If we have too much Yin, we become demotivated, and lazy. We miss out on the joy that new adventures can bring.

On the other hand, if we have too much yang, we become overstressed. We don't relax enough or cooperate enough, and this is extremely damaging to our health. We need to make sure that we balance the yin and yang in our bodies. Each of our organs has to be in balance.

For example, our brain scientists proved that our brain functions best when it has medium levels of stress. In other words, when Yin and Yang are at an equilibrium. We need both rest and stimulation in our lives.

Taoism honours the human body, comparing it sometimes with a country, the spirit being the king. As such, it must be administered and led very well, setting up what is acceptable, its rules of law and what it stands for.

To take leadership of anything in this world they have to first be able to take leadership of their own mind, body, and spirit. They have to be administered with excellence to implement the Taoist wisdom of the body in our lives. We need to apply practices like meditation, to slow down in our fast-paced modern world. This way we can learn to respect ourselves more, taking care of it in a more serious way to balance the Yin and Yang energies.

We need to organize our schedule, our relationships and our lives in such a way that we alternate intense periods of activity. Your Yang with relaxing periods of your Yin.

We need to sleep enough, eat/nourish well, and have satisfying relationships. But we also need to put ourselves out of our comfort zone by doing intense mental work at our jobs, or by performing intense physical activity or facing the inconvenience of speaking in public. For example, there is a great link between our body, our mental state, and our spirit. Taking care of our body means knowing how to balance our energy.

Our being in this balance leads to Zen a state of naturalness and happiness. Developing all of these full fundamental areas is mandatory. If we want to have a happy life, ignoring even one of them can lead to unhappiness. In other words, when a person is unhappy, this means that there is a dramatic lack in at least one of those four fundamental life areas.

If we ignore an area like self-development, our relationships can start to suffer because we're not capable of learning from our mistakes, and we continuously hurt other people. As a consequence, we'll become unhappy in time.

The wise thing to do is to schedule our week in such a way that we allocate enough time to reflect and work on each of the four areas in order to live a happy and fulfilling.

PUTTING IT ALL TOGETHER

To really start to implement this Taoist way of living I would love for you to consider three exercises. Past, Present, and Future.

Journaling Exercise #1 Reconciling with the Past
The Three Lists

List your family members and close friends.

Then another list of people you've hurt, and the third list of people who have hurt you.

The first list is the list of people you should take care of on a daily basis. Give them comfort and support them always, in both the good and bad times.

The second list is the list of people you should apologize to and try to repair the harm you caused them.

The last list is the list of people you must forgive, because resentment is poison, and it can cause more harm to you than to the person who harmed you.

Human beings are part of this cosmic force now. And the way we treat each other is basically the way we treat ourselves. Live in harmony with others. Take care of others as you would take care of yourself or a family member. Take care of your environment, and your life will become harmonious and peaceful.

Journaling & Self-Discovery Exercise.
The Present #2

Being able to identify the nature of what is in your life is the beginning of cleaning house. What is and what remains is your choice. Is it a necessary evil that comes with the territory but leads to your goal?

Nothing is good or bad. Everything is good and bad. As long as they serve a purpose towards your ultimate goal, every struggle, every challenge is part of your personal growth.

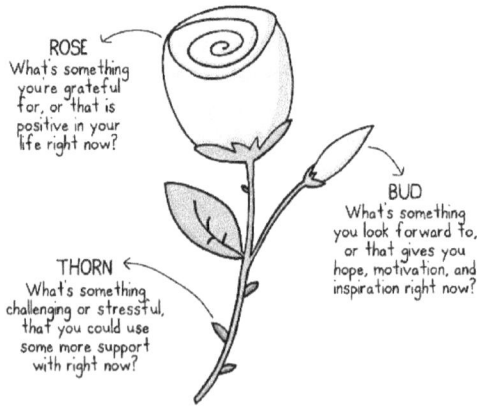

Journaling & Self-Discovery Exercise #3.
From now on...
6 words to help you set better boundaries

Setting stronger boundaries is central to strong leadership and your ability to reign as sovereign queen of your own life.

Think about it: having a border -- and lovingly protecting that border -- is what makes a nation a sovereign, independent nation. Whenever we travel, we always pass through border control. The officers are generally kind but firm (to me, anyway).

Kindness and firmness: the two greatest qualities of a boss boundary setter.

Chances are you need to set some boundaries in your own life right now. Maybe you need to delineate what you will and will not accept in your personal life or professional life. Perhaps you need to be clearer about what you will and will not tolerate from family members, clients, team members, etc.

In other words -- to reach your next level of success, you may need to become your own border control officer from time to time.

When that time comes, I have 6 words which -- when used in this exact order -- allow you to firmly and elegantly set boundaries, enforce them, and activate your power as sovereign queen of your own life and person.

Here they are: "That does not work for me."

A simple, straightforward phrase you can use anytime to firmly and respectfully set a boundary.

That does not work for me. No apology.

Instead... "but this will" after all,

every non-negotiable ought to have a

negotiable on your own terms.

ABOUT THE AUTHOR

Carolina Billings, PhD (C), MA-IS, CHRL, SHRP-SCP, CPCC is a social impact entrepreneur with 15+ year's leadership experience in the fields of Business Development, Leadership, Branding, Human Resources and Finance.

Carolina is the founder of Powerful Women Today, a boutique accelerator for success. A forum for the empowerment and optimization of women's status and lives.

Her sold-out conferences, publications, social impact, and Diversity, Inclusion & Equity initiatives have received the continued support and accolades of key champions of women in business. Carolina is proud to call herself an advocate working wholeheartedly for the emotional and financial independence and prosperity of women and their dependents.

Her Boutique Management Consulting Firm is comprised of elite experts championing women's growth. Her **#1MillionWomenChallenge** aims at positively impacting 1 Million Women every year to bring awareness to end violence against women and strengthen mental health and end financial dependency.

She is a leader with global impact who Champions and Empowers Women's Emotional and Financial Independence. She is proud of her adoptive home in Canada and is proud of her Hispanic heritage. She is a highly active advocate and champion of Social Justice, Diversity, Inclusion and Equity.

Carolina's dream is for every woman and little girl to realize that their uniqueness is their beauty and their talents their magic to love, touch lives, inspire others and shine brightest always.

CONTACT INFORMATION

Carolina M. Billings
carolina@powerfulwomentoday.com
https://www.linkedin.com/in/carolinabilings
https://www.powerfulwomentoday.com

Personal transformation can and does have global effects. As we go, so goes the world, for the world is us. The revolution that will save the world is ultimately a personal one.
Marianne Williamson

Dortha Hise

Dedication

To all who seek adventure.

And to my husband, Jason, who is always up for an adventure together.

CHAPTER 2

CHAMPIONING YOUR OWN ADVENTURE

FINDING JOY & ADVENTURE IN EVERY DAY

By Dortha Hise

The voicemail that changed my life

In the summer of 2012, I received a voice message that was the impetus to change my life… and not in a positive way, at least not at first.

The voicemail was from a stranger and he shared, in a very matter-of-fact fashion, that he regretted to inform me that "my mother had deceased." My mom and I had a challenging relationship which sparked off feelings that my grief process might also be challenging. I won't go into great detail about it here, however, I will tell you that she and I struggled to have a healthy relationship and over time, I learned that she was doing the best she could, and I was doing the best I could, and we struggled.

Upon my mom's passing, I felt a calling in my soul that I would write a book about this experience. I began with journaling.

I went out and spent time looking for what I felt was the perfect journal to begin this experience of complicated emotions. When I found the right journal, I gave myself permission to write in whatever form felt comfortable and share whatever felt like it needed to come to the surface. Oftentimes, I found myself feeling like I was reading myself. Other times like I was opening up a black hole of feelings and emotions and other experiences that have been explored more.

You see, what happened the summer of 2012 kicked off a 2-year period of loss and grief that would leave me with deep despair and heartache. At one point, the grief got so bad that I remember several nights that I would wake up in the middle of the night and touch my husband to make sure he was still breathing. I was scared to answer the phone, for the news on the other end might be that someone else had died.

A few months after the first series of people passed away, I was also diagnosed with a disorder that rendered my voice nearly a whisper. Another loss.

At the end of the two-year period I mentioned, I had lost 28 people from my life to various illnesses, accidents, and natural causes.

I was experiencing something I came to call "compounding grief" and I didn't know exactly how to process it. While in the midst of mourning the death of one person and I learned of someone else's passing, new grief would feel like it was piled on to the grief that I was already processing, muddying the experience and complicating the feelings and processing.

I had known I wanted to write a book about my journey, and I did self-publish a book called the **Rising Above the Ashes: Reigniting Your Joy After Any Loss.**

After all of the death I experienced, what had gone from writing a book about grieving the death of a parent or a relationship, where the relationship was complicated, changed to writing a book on reigniting joy after *any* loss, whether it was a companion, a spouse, a child, a pet, a business partner, a big client, etc...

Getting into nature

A year or so after my book came out my husband shared an invitation with me from a colleague to go on a three-day backpacking trip. I had always wanted to go backpacking... and living in the foothills that lead to the Sierra Nevada mountains seemed like an invitation to join this adventure.

We embarked on this three day, 44-mile backpacking trip, and at the onset of the trip I remember setting an intention to receive whatever I was meant to receive on this trip.

I kept an open mind on that intention throughout the entire trip.

I sat in silence a lot on this trip. Reflecting. Listening to inner wisdom come forth. Giving myself grace. I enjoyed the conversations with my husband and his colleague, who would become one of our closest friends over the years as a result of this and several other backpacking trips we took together.

When I returned home, I remember feeling incredible peace in my heart and in my soul. I couldn't put my finger on exactly what happened, only that the angst and heartache that I was feeling previously was gone

I've always been someone that has known the healing power of nature. I believe the trip was the opening of my allowing whatever I was meant to receive by way of healing or moving forward in all of my grief, or closing chapters of my life in the past to come forward and take full effect.

Being Open to Receive

Sometimes being open to receive can appear in ways that you don't anticipate.

For example, receiving peace about a situation where there was struggle previously.

Or perhaps it comes in allowing yourself permission to receive.

Being gentle with yourself throughout the process is a necessary step in order to allow what will come to show up.

And while it may sound like I'm speaking in riddles or circles about receiving as a magical thing that which will render itself with a beacon and a strobe light somewhere, it's not that. Sometimes the inner things that we work on don't show up in a physical manifestation of a "thing," rather as peace or calmness, or satisfaction, etc.

Sometimes the gift of receiving is in that openness to receive it.

Championing Your Own Adventure

While I'm certainly an advocate for getting outdoors, it doesn't have to be something as extreme as doing a multi-day backpacking trip... here are five ways to champion your own adventure today:

- **Earthing or grounding** – take your shoes off and put your feet into the dirt. Rub your feet into the dirt if you can. The energetic exchange of your feet and the earth can do wonders for our well-being.
- **Hug a tree** – yes, seriously. There is scientific proof that hugging a tree is good for us. There is an exchange of our negative ions and the tree's positive ions that can invoke feelings of happiness from the release of the hormone oxytocin, while also having an effect on reducing stress. Yes, please!
- **Watch the clouds** – Can you remember when you were a kid and you laid down in the grass and made shapes out of the passing clouds? Not only is watching the clouds great for our imagination, but it can also enhance our mental state.
- **Start a nature journal** – this can be an incredibly cathartic and fun way to explore the nature around you while documenting things you see in your area. Grab a notebook and pen and head to a local park, trail, or forest and take note of the birds you see, different flowers you see, different textures of tree bark, etc. Consider jotting notes down about

how you feel as you allow each of your senses to experience this time in nature.

- ❖ **Spend time by a body of water** – water is incredibly cathartic and sitting by a river, lake, creek, or even a pool can be soothing. Water cleanses, and as it does in nature and has for millennia, if you are open to receiving the gifts that being near a body of water can provide, perhaps you can also receive cleansing. If you're feeling particularly adventurous and it is safe (and permissible) to do so, consider jumping into the water... ahhh! Invigorating!

> *"Grab a notebook and pen and head to a local park, trail, or forest and take note of the birds you see, different flowers you see, different textures of tree bark, etc. Consider jotting notes down about how you feel as you allow each of your senses to experience this time in nature."*

If you are reading this and thinking "Yeah, Dortha, and I don't live close to a National Park or forest to go for a hike or get quality time in nature... so what can I do?" Here are some suggestions to get out and enjoy nature:

- Sit in your backyard and enjoy the sound of the birds
- Walk to a local park and take in the scenery
- Plant a tree (or find an organization that you can volunteer with and plant several trees)
- Watch the sunrise
- Watch the moonrise (bonus points for finding the limited window of time when the sun is setting and the moon is rising!)
- Drink a hot tea or chocolate in the snow
- Look for four-leaf clovers in your yard
- Stop and smell the roses… or petunias, or whatever might be around your neighborhood.
- Take a walk after work (or on your lunch break)
- Make a meal and eat it outside

You get the idea, right? The options are endless and really bound only by your imagination! Have a partner or spouse? Get their input, too. Have kids? Get them involved in the process, too!

Putting it All Together, Doing the Work, and Healing

As I mentioned at the beginning of this chapter, the phone call I received that afternoon in the summer of 2012 was the impetus to change my life, and not in a positive way, at first.

I never would have thought that grief could have carved the transformational journey in my life that it has.

During my journey, I made a conscious effort to tell myself that this grief I was experiencing wasn't what defined me. It was part of who I am… not all of me.

I chose to look for the light at the end of the tunnel, even when the shit seemed to be hitting the fan and blocking the light, or evaporating what little light I could see entirely.

It took work. A lot of work. I got to explore options that didn't work for me, while finding and embracing ones that did.

I chose to do the work.

It was ugly. It was messy. I cried a lot. I also laughed a lot. I was gentle with myself for the most part. I also found that I would get into a spiral from time-to-time and beat myself up. When I noticed those feelings showing up, I gave myself permission to show up as my authentic self and to have grace in those moments.

- ❖ The healing has been a continued and ongoing journey.
- ❖ Every backpacking trip we go on, I set the same intention as I did our first trip.
- ❖ I continue to be open to receive what I am meant to receive.
- ❖ I lean into curiosity and ask questions.
- ❖ I continue to have grace with myself.
- ❖ I continue to show up authentically as myself.
- ❖ I continue to heal.

And I encourage you to do the same in championing for your own adventures as well. I will leave you with a few tips for being gracious with yourself on this journey:

- ❖ Be gentle with yourself – you are doing the best you can
- ❖ Celebrate your wins – all of the wins, big and small
- ❖ Document your journey – whether you journal or choose another way to document, getting

thoughts out of your head and onto paper is a powerful experience.

ABOUT THE AUTHOR

Dortha Hise is the COE (Chief Overwhelm Eliminator) of Pretty Smart Virtual Services, a full-service virtual assistant company specializing in rescuing their clients from overwhelm. She is also the Director of Adventure at Summit to Your Success, a choose-your-own-adventure-focused healing portal where she helps others to learn about the healing power of nature. Dortha loves helping her clients to choose their own adventures by freeing them up from their to-do lists.

After enduring multiple devastating personal losses during a 2-year period, Dortha also lost her voice. She thought it was a simple case of laryngitis or bronchitis…as it turns out, it was not simple… it took several doctor visits, specialists, and other non-traditional medical visits to be diagnosed with a neurological condition called Abductor Spasmodic Dysphonia ("AB SD").

AB SD prevented Dortha from using the phone or speaking normally or being easily heard in a room with a lot of ambient noise. While this presented challenges to Dortha, she is grateful for this experience as it has heightened her sense of hearing and it allows her to really hone in on what others are saying (or perhaps not saying).

Always the positive thought leader, Dortha began to fully understand the mindset of high achievers. Her ability to optimize businesses and operations helped leaders in their businesses but she observed the overwhelm did not always go away.

After going on a 3-day backpacking trip in 2015 and was able to fully experience the healing power that nature had to offer. She set an intention to be open to whatever she was meant to receive on the trip and when she returned home, she felt a very strong sense of peace around the difficult relationship she had with her mom, and the grief she was struggling to process became easier to release.

She is now teaching others to do the same in her Choose Your Own Adventure Healing Portal bringing about full mind shifts and personal transformation of those who lead helping them serve the world at their best.

CONTACT INFORMATION

Dortha Hise
Founder, Pretty Smart Virtual Services
Founder, Summit to Your Success
https://prettysmartvaservices.com/
https://natureguidestoselfhealing.com/
https://www.linkedin.com/in/dorthahise/

"May the next few months be a period of magnificent transformation."
Anonymous

Kim Ward

Dedication

To every woman who feels like she should give up; don't stop now. It's beautiful on the other side!

To my husband Richard- You've been my best friend, my biggest cheerleader and the parachute to all of my jumps! If it weren't for your endless support we wouldn't be where we are. I love you always!

CHAPTER 3

THE 5 SECRETS OF TRANS-FLOW-MATION

By Kim Ward

I dropped out of high school in 11th grade, but I'm not un or under-educated. I know that "transflowmation" isn't a word and you'll soon understand that transflowmation is a journey.

February of the year 2000 was an extremely cold month in Massachusetts, but that didn't stop me. I was 17 years old, and I had to figure out why I was getting nauseous and throwing up after eating. My mother was a single mother working as a grocery store cashier. We had no car, no money, not much of anything, so I knew that if I was going to get to the doctor for answers, I was on my own.

I wrapped my warmest coat around my body and started the very long walk in the blistering cold wind across town to the urgent care facility. Urgent care was my only choice. For one, we didn't have a family doctor and two, they couldn't turn me away for not having insurance.

When it was my turn to be seen the female doctor looked at me and asked, *"When was your last period?"*

I honestly didn't know.

That wasn't something I tracked. I was self-taught up to this point, so I just kind of knew when they were coming but never really stopped to think about them...not coming.

Tilting my head to recall, I blurted out *"December?"* As if I were asking the doctor. She was very clearly annoyed, and it was as if she had seen this play out a million times in her career. Rolling her eyes, she handed me a plastic specimen cup and shooed me across the hall to collect a urine sample.

I handed her the cup and in a very agitated manner she snatched it from me. It took less than

5 seconds for her to shout *"Well, that was the quickest positive I've ever seen!"*

Still not catching on, I looked up from staring at the wall and asked, *"What do you mean?"*

"You're pregnant!" She scolded.

Time stopped. My breathing stopped. I just stared in disbelief. I was 8 weeks pregnant with the size of a kidney bean causing all the sickness.

> *"Life is what happens to you while you're busy making other plans."*
> *-John Lennon*

You've heard stories about moms with an insane amount of Adrenaline lifting cars off their baby; that's how I felt. Something inside of me switched immediately and forever.

Why do I tell you this?

Sometimes we need adversity in order to shift us, wake us up from the autopilot trans that we're in. For me, that boy changed my life. I went back to school, received my diploma and passed a 3 month Phlebotomy course at my local community college with a 97% final grade.

> *"Challenge is nothing more than a seed of opportunity."*

I was offered a full-time job at a well-known Boston hospital and started working my way up the chain. Within 4 years, I was offered the position of lead phlebotomist and a year after that I was offered the role of phlebotomy supervisor. Now, as the youngest supervisor in the entire New England region for my company, I was supervising individuals who were once my peers. It was a big challenge, but one worth growing through. You see, most of us want transformation but without the discomfort.

My success was based on communication, on listening and letting people know that I cared. That's when I realized **secret #1**: Helping others achieve their goals was helping me achieve mine.

I had adopted this department of misfits but through building trust, communicating on a regular basis, helping them develop a success blueprint, I was molding a well oiled machine. Our metrics improved, we were seeing less errors, patients were happier visiting our department and employees were happier being at work. My superiors took notice, as did the physicians and staff that we served, so I was offered the role of phlebotomy manager with a stipulation. I had to get my Bachelor's degree. So, I did.

The company had a tuition reimbursement program and I took full advantage. I went back to school as a full time mom with a full time job and went through the accelerated courses online. In roughly 2 years, I had my bachelor's degree, a new job as a phlebotomy manager, a $5,000 sign on bonus with full benefits and a company car that I was allowed to use for personal use.

My son and I were thriving, until I realized that I was miserable. I had achieved absolutely everything that I had worked so hard for, but had I? Had something shifted inside of me again?

Yeah, it sure did!

I was dropping my child off at before school services and sending him to after school services just so I could be at work. He was literally in someone else's care for about 10 hours a day. I was home for dinner, bath, and bed. It was heart breaking and there was no balance of work and life. It was all work, and the weekends were for laundry, grocery shopping and house cleaning.

Secret #2: You can't live your life for the opinions and expectations of others.

Being a teenage mom and a high school drop out meant that I had something to prove to the world, but it was costing me precious time with my son that I would never get back. I was chasing titles and money and certainly not enjoying it enough just for the "look what I've done with my life" bragging rights.

Secret #3: Do what makes you happy! End of story.

9 short years into my career, I quit. I gave my notice with no job to fall back on. I knew what I wanted, and it would have to be created.

> *"A single dream is more powerful than a thousand realities."*
> *- J.R.R. Tolkien*

Entrepreneurship offered time, freedom, financial independence and the ability to work from anywhere. I opened my laptop and just like that, I had started an online business.

For 4 months I posted about my business and wondered why I hadn't made any sales. My ego was saying that because it was me, everyone should know better, take my word for it, and buy my stuff. It was time for another transformation.

It dawned on me that everything I had learned and applied in my corporate positions needed to be explored in my new role as an entrepreneur. I used my communication skills to network on social media. I listened to people, I heard the pains and problems in their life and when my business made sense to their situation, I offered it as a solution.

With this new approach, I grew my business to $17,000/month in sales within a few months. Fear crept in though.

Can I maintain this?

What happens if I hit major success?

All of the limiting beliefs rolled in like thunder clouds and I found myself sabotaging my own efforts. Before long, my sales had dwindled down to a few hundred dollars a month. In my mind, it was easier to start a new business than resurrect a dead or dying one, so once again, I built a new business.

This time it didn't take me months to be in profit. It was within 30 days.

This cycle of sabotage, self-abuse and ups and downs went on for 4 years. Something had to give. I needed lasting transformation because it wasn't the businesses that were failing, it was still me trying to prove to the world that I was more than a teenage statistic.

Mindset and personal growth became a new part of my days. I learned about afformations. Don't confuse this with affirmation. Affirmations are a positive sentence, but what happens when you read or write a sentence that your brain knows is a lie?

You: "I am easily making $10,000 a month"

Your brain: "Um, NO you're not!"

Here's **secret #4**: Each morning, start your day with one powerful question that only has a positive outcome. Mine was "How can I show up more powerfully today?" This question is called an afformation. It's not a lie and your brain will be determined to find an answer for this question. Before you know it, you will start to behave in a way that solves this question.

It took me a year and a half to build a global, multiple six-figure business from home. I was living my dream of time, freedom, financial independence, and impacting so many people, starting in my own home.

Secret #5: Have a vision.

If you don't have a clear vision, how do you know where you're going? If you're not going somewhere intentionally, it's the same as rolling out of bed and just letting the day happen to you. And I can tell you - nothing is by accident, but it's better if you're in the driver's seat of your life and not a backseat driver.

Live loud, live bold and live with purpose! I now have 3 beautiful children, a husband that I love and adore. My business retired him after 23 years of fire-rescue service. We founded a nonprofit organization for mental health awareness, I am a 3X best-selling author, and if this high school dropout is telling you that transformation is possible; You've got this...

Transflowmation = Going with the flow intentionally and with purpose.

ABOUT THE AUTHOR

Kim Ward is a warrior who wears many hats. As a mental health advocate, a suicide attempt survivor & a multiple suicide loss survivor, Kim is the founder & CEO of Katie's Mission, a nonprofit organization for mental health awareness.

As a digital marketing strategist, Kim helps entrepreneurs and small businesses leverage the power of social media so they can comfortably build a profitable business without missing out on other important areas of their life.

Kim is a 3X best-selling author, a mom to 3 beautiful humans, caregiver to her father & has retired her husband and partner, Rich after serving as a first responder for 23 years.

www.powerfulwomentoday.com

CONTACT INFORMATION

Kim Ward
Kim@lifebydesignsolutions.com
http://www.SuccessWithKimWard.com

The most alluring thing a woman can have is confidence." Beyonce Knowles

Stacey Hall

Dedication

I dedicate this book to everyone who chooses to make life an on-going transformational experience.

CHAPTER 4

10 TINY TRANSFORMATIONS THAT CREATE AN ABUNDANTLY PROSPEROUS LIFE

By Stacey Hall

During my early adulthood, I was often a negative person, having grown up in a household that focused on what was wrong… instead of what was good in our lives.

I was eventually introduced to the concept that we manifest what we focus upon, and I realized that I could change my outlook through focused effort and attention. I made a pact with myself to create a set of tools and resources – tiny transformations -- that I would use every day to keep my physical, emotional, mental, and spiritual energy as abundantly high as possible. I call these tools and resources my 'Energy Surges' because they boost my attitude up to the highest heights of positivity and prosperity.

> *"I made a pact with myself to create a set of tools and resources – tiny transformations -- that I would use every day"*

These are my 10 'Energy Surges':

Energy Surge #1: Scheduling for Success

The extent to which a goal can be fulfilled is dependent upon the amount of intention that is committed towards the achievement of that goal. An "intention" is the commitment to achieve the goal. All the planned conversations, activities, meetings, and projects we schedule are intentional activities. Each one will have a 'by when' date attached to it so that the goal can be achieved as quickly as possible.

It is much easier to have a positive and prosperous outlook when we move forward towards the achievement of our goals.

Energy Surge #2: Do It Your Way Any Way You Can

I heard master motivator Zig Ziglar state this truth in the 1990's at an empowerment seminar and it changed my life in that moment. Up to that point, I was a perfectionist. If I could not do something right the first time...I simply would not even attempt to do it. Yet, upon hearing Zig's amazing, transformative statement: *"Anything worth doing is worth doing poorly...the first time,"* I began experimenting, playing, researching, or asking for help...anything that would help me to take the first step poorly on my way to discovering how to do it perfectly.

I gave a TEDx presentation on how to do it 'your way'. I invite you to watch on Youtube at http://snip.ly/xtkmo

---

It is much easier to have a positive and prosperous outlook when we feel free to experiment and make mistakes as we learn.

Energy Surge #3: Tending to Your Goals Garden

I love the concept of achieving goals in the same way that we grow a garden. The cycle is Seeding, Sprouting, Blooming and Resting. This is a consistent *Energy Surge* – a reminder that while I focus on achieving a goal – such as *becoming a positive person* -- I am going to move through a cycle of discovery and growth.

It is much easier to have a positive and prosperous outlook when we are not pushing the goal to bloom before its time!

Energy Surge #4: Surround Your Self with Positive People

If we are truly committed to being a positive person, then it is up to us to seek out and spend as much time as possible with positive people so that our outlook becomes more positive. At one time, I had very few friends that I considered to be positive people. I chose to change my situation. I am fortunate that my husband always has a positive view of the world or can find humor in any situation. I chose to spend as much time as possible with him. I chose to watch 'The Ellen Show' every day at 3:00 p.m. because I knew her positive humor would make me laugh. I found a positive-thinking hair stylist, nail technician, massage therapist, doctor, etc. And I also started hanging out in positive-focused groups on Facebook, Meetup, and Google. I now have a wide circle of positive-thinking friends with whom I have mutually beneficial and supportive relationships.

I recorded a free video coaching session for you on how to be immune to the opinions and actions of others. It's on Youtube at http://snip.ly/q9477

"It is much easier to be a positive person who attracts greater prosperity when there is no room for negative people in our life."

Energy Surge #5: Read and Practice 'The 4 Agreements' by don Miguel Ruiz

I was so empowered by reading **The Four Agreements**® by don Miguel Ruiz, I chose to consciously practice each of the Agreements in every conversation – written and/or verbal -- I have with others to create more harmonious relationships. In doing so, I have a stronger and more loving relationship with myself, which creates a positive outlook on my life.

It is much easier to be a positive and prosperity-minded person when we are "impeccable with our word" (Agreement #1), we don't make assumptions (Agreement #2), we don't take things personally (Agreement #3), and we do our best in each moment (Agreement #4)

Energy Surge #6: Show Love and Appreciation to Others and to Our Self

All too often, when we focus our attention on what others 'have' and we do not, we fall into a state of negative thinking. Comparison and desire can lead to frustration and envy. Now I only focus on my 'haves'! The practice of acknowledging and appreciating what I already have brings me more of what I desire simply, easily and with velocity.

This includes showing appreciation to the people in my life who engage in positive conversations with me, who contribute to my well-being and my prosperity. I discovered, the more I express appreciation to the people in my life, the happier I am, and I can see a direct correlation to an increase in appreciation I receive in return.

I recorded a free video coaching session for you on how to attract more appreciation. Watch it at http://snip.ly/grm2a

---

It is much easier to be a positive and prosperous-minded person when we are feeling appreciated.

Energy Surge #7: Release all 'Shoulds' and Obligations

Whenever I share this *Energy Surge* with others, they usually say, "Easier said than done." I agree.

Yet, the more I stop 'shoulding' on myself, the happier and more productive I become. I've chosen to accept that just because someone asks me to do something, does not mean I must say 'yes.'

If I truly choose to accept someone's request because it will make me happy if I do, then I will do it. Otherwise, I choose not to do it.

To ensure I don't feel guilty about my decision, I have created this personal affirmation:

"My body is a temple. I clear and clean my body, heart, and soul. I lovingly and willingly release all that no longer serves me in a positive and progressive way. I now attract inspiring, enjoyable

people, places, and events into my life! I trust all of my needs are met as they arise all the time.

I recorded a free video coaching session about how to say 'No' without feeling guilty. Watch at http://snip.ly/dkw1r

---

> *"It is much easier to be a positive person when I keep my physical, emotional, mental, and spiritual environment clear and free of 'shoulds.'*

Energy Surge #8: Take Regular Rest Stops

So many people feel that the only way to achieve their goals is to keep push, push, pushing their way to the top. I used to be one of them.

Each day would be filled with as many activities as I could cram in before I collapsed into bed from exhaustion.

Back then, I prided myself on 'beating the clock' by accomplishing as much as possible before time ran out. And, eventually it did run out!

I was unable to sustain my success. Because I was not eating well, my physical body ran out of energy and my mental creativity ran dry. Because I was not loving myself, I became resentful of what I was giving to others.

Under doctor's orders, I was put on complete bed rest…which lasted 2 years…to replenish, re-nourish, and recuperate.

It was difficult for me at the beginning of this period because I felt like I was being lazy and not being of service to others.

One of the few enjoyments of my recuperation process was listening to music…and I became aware of how a song is composed of both notes and rest stops…and how the music is created by the spaces between the notes.

I realized that I was experiencing my own rest stop in the symphony of my life.

I realized that, as much as it appeared I was doing 'nothing,' I was actually doing the most important work of all. I was creating a beautiful harmony between **doing** and **resting** to keep my energy fully charged to be able to attain and *sustain* success!

When I stopped resisting the process of resting, I began to recover quickly. That was more than 10 years ago.

Now, I schedule rest stops in-between each meeting, phone call, social media project, and every other activity I have each day to ensure my life continues to be a beautiful symphony of productivity.

It is much easier to be a positive and prosperity-minded person when all 4 of our bodies feel rested.

Energy Surge #9: Make the 'Best Feeling' Choices

Most people become confused as soon as a decision or a choice arises which they must make. They stop to reflect on possible outcomes, yet the longer they dwell on their choices, the more confused they become. Attempting to release their selves from their confusion, they start asking other people these 4 dis-empowering words:

"What Should I Do?"

When we ask someone else to tell us what to do, we have abdicated our own power. That is what I did all the time until the day I remembered most -- if not all -- spiritual belief systems are based on the concept that the two most powerful energies are 'love' and 'fear.' Love is the harmonizing empowering force of nature while Fear is the exact opposite. Therefore, decisions made from Love will be quite different than those based on Fear. You may wish to take a moment now to consider a decision you made recently. Did you base your decision on the principle of *Love* or was your decision generated from *Fear*?

It is much easier to be a positive and prosperity-minded person when we feel our decisions are energizing and empowering and support us to take an action from a sense of desire, passion, commitment, and/or intention.

Energy Surge #10: Be Accountable to Be a Positive and Prosperity-Minded Person

The day I chose to 'count on' myself to be a positive person with a prosperity outlook was the day I started to become that person. I gave up 'wishing' and 'hoping' by choosing to be 'Personally Accountable' to myself. I chose to commit to specific behaviors, actions, and thoughts – these same 10 tiny transformations. I have become a person with a positive and prosperous outlook on life.

It is much easier to be a positive and prosperity-minded person when we practice these 10 Energy Surges!

ABOUT THE AUTHOR

My passion is to help women entrepreneurs, who feel frustrated they have not been able to make the difference for others they want to make. My 'Go For YES' fun 4-step formula makes it possible for them to attract their ideal audience, solve the problems of their audience, increase their income, and leave a positive legacy that lives on long after they are gone.

CONTACT INFORMATION

Stacey Hall
Facebook: https://www.facebook.com/staceyhall1
LinkedIn: https://www.linkedin.com/in/staceyhall1/

*This world's not going to change unless we're
willing to change ourselves.*
Rigoberta Menchu

Leona Krasner

Dedication

To my little Aureli

CHAPTER 5

NEW BABY AND ME

THE TRANSFORMATIONAL EFFECT OF A LITTLE ONE ON HEALTH, WORK, AND RELATIONSHIPS

By Leona Krasaner

The term "giving birth" is often thrown around loosely, particularly in business circles. What entrepreneur doesn't feel the magic of the creation of something brand new? Songwriters birth songs, and sculptors' birth artistic feats, but rarely is actual, biological birth a part of the conversation in mainstream society. I believe it should be.

My baby boy was born four months ago, and he has simultaneously turned my life upside down and crystalized what was most important for me: keeping this wondrous, tiny little boy with ever-growing cheeks fed, clean, happy, and content. A personal development junkie, I immediately set to work determining what my goals would be in the areas of my health, work, and relationships, and then re-assessed each in light of my trusty baby sidekick. I am excited to share my transformational takeaways in each of these areas with you.

Health

I admit it. I thought that being pregnant would be a breeze, that childbirth would be just fine, the natural, unmedicated way that women have been doing it for millennia, and that I would bounce right back to my pre-pregnant weight immediately, because hello, breastfeeding. Things didn't quite work out that way.

A quick preface about me – I love goals. More specifically, I love crushing them. And so, I made goals around conceiving, birthing, and my body. One constant theme that I came to truly respect is the idea of giving myself grace - the permission to forgive myself for not quite reaching those lofty goals, but instead either landing somewhere close, or somewhere even better.

As a pregnant woman, I adored bread. And potatoes, and basically any and every kind of dairy that I was permitted to eat. All of my life, my mother told me again and again how she only gained twenty pounds with me, and she lost all twenty the moment I popped out of her. Especially in those last days of pregnancy, having gained over forty pounds, I counted down the days until I would meet my little one, and also be able to fit into my form-fitting tea party dresses. Spoiler alert – four months later, I still do not fit into those tea dresses, but my body produces the food my baby needs to flourish, and those dresses (and jeans) can wait. Being able to properly provide for my baby, as only a mother can, has taken such greater priority over the clothes that I will one day fit into that it's not even funny.

Ah, pregnancy. I was convinced that I, like my foremothers before me, would have an easy go of it. Contractions hit three days before I actually gave birth, and my baby was perfectly comfy to just stay in my tummy a few days past his due date, thank you very much. I did the sideways walking.

I did the room temperature bath with the OBGYN-approved bath salts from Whole Foods (room temperature baths suck). I downloaded the app that timed my contractions. But I was determined to do this thing unmedicated. And then I got to the hospital. The contractions did not let up, but it was four hours before I allowed myself to deviate from my plan. I got the epidural. After 4 jabs in the wrong part of my back, the blessed relief I felt at finally getting a chance to let out a deep breath is indescribable. I pave my own way, and I am allowed to change my mind. That was a revelation. I don't have to do it as others have before me. I've always known this to be true in the business world, and in the networking world, but this idea applied even more so in the delivery world.

Another of the bigger revelations upon becoming a mommy was how finnicky this whole making breast milk thing really is. Turns out I had to eat way more post-popping out baby than I ever did while pregnant, which blew me away. Even more surprising – "healthy eating," such as only having a salad or a smoothie, would completely eviscerate my next pumping session. Apparently, it was well-balanced eating, complete with flour, grains, and carbs, that helped up those ounces of breast milk that I produced.

Stress was one more surprise area as it related to breast milk production – it absolutely tanked milk supply! I needed to figure out stress-busting techniques, and fast. My husband really helped me with this one. Getting the stressful, annoying, scary, anger-inducing stuff out of my head, whether just by telling my husband about it or writing it all down, served to instantly take a huge amount of pressure off. Once the fretting about it part was done, I could do something about it, putting me in the driver's seat. Now, even texting my husband about something that's bothering me serves to make me feel better, because I know that I will get to explain in far further detail that evening.

In short, by growing and having my baby, I re-evaluated my health by looking through the lens of how I can best provide for my son. I gave myself permission to take charge of what my baby's birth would look like and how I would get there, regardless of what others close to me had done. Once baby was out, I transformed my definition of healthy eating so that I could best provide for him.

Work

Baby-making and work. What an adventure. From the get-go, I knew I would go back to work sooner rather than later after baby boy was born. The moment he was out, however, I knew the focus would have to be on him. The key was reprioritizing my life such that baby was front and center.

I am the Founder and Managing Partner of a ten-employee law firm that helps folks in New York and New Jersey with their family law needs. I had two key goals as they related to work and my baby:

1. My baby would be nourished almost fully with my milk; and

2.   I wanted to maximize my time with my little love to the greatest degree I could.

The regular, insurance-covered pump meant I was a prisoner to the closest wall with an outlet, and I would need both hands to do this, one to hold the pump part to my breast, and the other to hold the bottle. I was shocked by the old-fashionedness of this process. Surely, something had been invented that could help women continue to serve as members of the 21st century while still pumping. A few conversations and one wireless pump purchase later, and I became the proud, relieved owner of a set of devices that let me travel to bathrooms throughout courthouses in New York and New Jersey galore in order to pump. One place that became almost a pumping haven for me was Uber rides to and from the courthouse. I could pump, speak to clients, opposing counsel, and employees, all while providing for my baby, conveniently under a nursing cover. The flexibility to ensure that I could pump enough and on my own schedule was there; I just had to do the legwork to make it happen.

Breastfeeding turned out to be one of the most counterintuitive things I had ever experienced. Turns out you don't just stick the pointy end into the baby's mouth and let him do what he needs to do. I am still convinced that my child's first word will be "bigger," since that was the main thing I was telling him for the first weeks. We had to make sure his latch was big enough that he was getting enough milk and wasn't hurting me while he breastfed.

As I returned to work, I thought hard regarding when I could get in time with my cutie. A big chunk of time during the workday couldn't work, because of the unpredictability of my court schedule. I settled on early mornings, as soon as he woke up, evenings from 5:30 – 7:00 pm, around his bedtime, and Saturdays and Sundays. These evening times and weekends in particular have become my safe havens to love on my little honey, have adventures with him, and get in much needed us time. These times and days have also become my favorite parts of the day and week. Getting to see that little face, wide gummy smile, and those kicking feet is everything. No matter how hard the day, knowing that my little boy needs me, loves me, and is so gosh darn happy to see me floors me every time.

Relationships

People talk about how much of a burden a new baby puts on a relationship. Heck, I see it in my law practice all the time. But surely that wouldn't happen to me.

Turns out that caring for a whole new human, coupled with way less sleep than we had ever had before, meant that the pressure hit us, even though I did not expect it to do so. Communication was key. My husband asking me in those first post-birth days how I was feeling, really, made such a difference. Taking the time over dinner, or whichever five-minute meal we could grab before baby let us know he was up again, to share our worries, best practices, latest internet or Facebook mommy group discoveries we had learned, and plan together, made all the difference. It was when one of us shut down or bottled up that would hurt us the most.

So, we continue to have a nightly dinner together, where we discuss our day. My lovely husband continues to brew the most perfect cup of coffee each morning, with a few sips for me, of course. We continue to do relationship review every Sunday evening, sharing with the other all of the ways the other went above and beyond, specific instances of what could have gone better, and what we need to do so that those incidents never happen again. We continue to do all we can to find things to giggle about, be they poopy explosions or how baby's latest night swaddle makes him look like an astronaut. Most importantly, we continue to give each other grace, more than ever before, understanding that this child-rearing thing is a first for both of us.

Regarding relationships that are not between my husband and myself, we have gotten better and better at boundary-setting. The perspective that our child will be learning and soaking in words, behaviors, and even potentially beliefs from those with whom we surround him have made us very selective about who we permit into our inner circle. I only wanted my husband present during our baby's birth, and so we conveniently forgot to tell everyone that we were on our way to the hospital and only mentioned it to our closest people once baby was born. We are just too busy for certain folks at this stage in baby's life. With some others, we only go for walks together. What is key is that my husband and I control the narrative, and no one gets to change it but us. It is our duty to instill in our son the morals and values that will guide him through his life, and one big place he will learn those is by the company we keep.

Conclusions

Having a real baby, as opposed to my business baby, or any other kind of entrepreneurial project, has been the most life-changing thing to ever occur for me. Becoming a mum has served to make my life that much richer, more colorful, and certainly more full of gorgeous sunrises for which I am now awake, feeding my love.

The lessons that have made the biggest impact on my life after having a baby are:

- ❖ You are the boss. Even with a peeing, pooing, burping, drooling, spit-upping little one, you still wield the paintbrush of your life.
- ❖ Let it out. Share the feelings, the worries, the hurt, the annoyances, so that they are out of your system, and you can focus on the beauty of a little hand holding your finger, a brand new little noise, a smile, or a giggle.
- ❖ Give yourself grace when you don't knock out absolutely every single item on the list. You made a baby. That should top every single list you create from here-on in.
- ❖ Communicate. Make clear what does and does not work for you. It'll be hard sometimes from so little sleep, but be as clear and articulate as possible about what is and is not serving you.

ABOUT THE AUTHOR

Leona S. Krasner, Esq., MBA, first became interested in relationships and justice at the age of seven, when she decided to become an attorney. As she studied the Social Sciences, her major at Brooklyn Technical High School, and then went on to double major in Psychology and Politics at New York University, her interest in relationships and justice only grew. Her studies at Washington and Lee University School of Law, where she earned her Juris Doctorate, and then at the Stern School of Business at New York University, where she earned her Master's of Business Administration, shaped her decision to pursue the law, and then start her own law firm. Today, Leona is the Managing Partner of Krasner Law, PLLC, a family law firm that helps folks in New York and New Jersey get married, stop being married, and help with the children, too. Her boutique law firm is quickly expanding, and she currently has twelve employees. When not assisting clients with their family law issues, Leona regularly posts relationship tips across social media. Her ideology is that she would love to help people strengthen their relationships, if at all possible. If that doesn't work, she and her firm stand ready to assist.

When not practicing law, Leona helps students as Managing Director of Krasner Review, LLC, a tutoring company that assists students with standardized examination preparation, application preparation, and scholarship negotiation. She also enjoys managing and performing at concerts that she puts on as Managing Director of her nonprofit organization, Tunes for Tots & Teens, through which volunteer musicians play concerts for children. She also enjoys going on adventures with her husband, traveling, and reading.

CONTACT INFORMATION

Leona S. Krasner, Esq., MBA
Krasner Law, PLLC
Leona@lkrasner.com | www.lkrasner.com
https://www.linkedin.com/in/leonakrasner/

"Strong women don't have 'attitudes',
we have standards."
Marylin Monroe

Stephaney Campbell

Dedication

To all the amazing people in my life who inspired and shaped my journey.
I owe it all to one woman and a force to be reckoned with, my mother Lorna Bryan, my guiding star and strength. I will continue to make you proud. Words can not express how much I and every life you blessed and transformed misses you.

CHAPTER 6

FROM "YES" TO "FOREVER" (THE EMPOWERED COUPLE)

By Stephaney Campbell

Key points:

- ❖ The importance of marriage preparation
- ❖ Building a foundation and future
- ❖ You're a team... Setting healthy boundaries with family and friends
- ❖ Standing together as an empowered couple

You have found your life partner; without a shadow of a doubt this is your forever person. Marriage is on the horizon, and you're excited to walk down the aisle and begin your life together. However, with this joyous occasion comes much thought and responsibility. The person you decide to say "I do" to will inevitably change the course of your life, positively or negatively. When this transformation begins, I have a few golden nuggets to help make the transition lasting and empowering.

Many couples may underestimate the power of marriage preparation. Some couples are even reluctant to the idea as they may feel it to be an outdated practice. As the saying goes "An ounce of prevention is worth a pound of cure".

Whether you're newly engaged, planning your wedding day, or have been married for years, it can come as a shock for couples to experience challenges, disagreements, and struggles in their relationships. All too often, couples approach the big day with the assumption that the marriage of fairy tales will be theirs, that their love will always be enough, and that maintaining their relationship while taking care of themselves as individuals will be easy.

As wonderful as that may sound, all couples face challenges. Now we have created a plan to help couples build that foundation. My brilliant mentor, Hailey Party-founder of the Happy Love marriage preparation workshop, has taught me how to guide couples and help them insulate their marriages using 5 essential steps to creating an IDEAL marriage. This method has helped me in my relationship, as well as in the couples I have coached.

Building a strong foundation as a couple is essential to any relationship. A part of creating the ideal love is taking inventory of where you are now, designing the version of the love you want, eliminating roadblocks, creating an action plan, and learning the 6 skills of happy couples. There are many areas of a relationship to consider. Your financial landscape, spousal health, communication, parenting, trust, and division of labor, are a few topics high on the list.

When my now husband and I announced to our family and friends we were getting married, one of the most repeated statements we heard was "marriage takes work," and no one ever really mentioned what that work was other than the timeless classic "happy wife, happy life".

We took the advice with a grain of salt since we were a couple for 8 years before his proposal and share a son. As the second chapter of my dear friend and mentor Hailey's book "Happy Love" says "There's hidden dirt in your relationship". Well sure enough that dirt resurfaced in the form of resentment of adult children from my husband's previous marriage and family and friends inserting their 2 cents, a few examples from my personal experience. For others, it can be dealing with financial hardships, infidelity, sex, fun/adventure, or even a spouse's health issue.

As for me, I was getting weary and losing hope and vision. My husband, being a mild-mannered and non-confrontational person, was trying to please too many people at once. Couples can get lost in all the outside noise and unsolicited opinions. Building a foundation and setting life goals together is one half of the equation. Being a team and working together is just as important, seeing your partner as your ally in healing fosters an evolution beyond what you could have imagined in the beginning. When we prioritize our partner and set healthy boundaries, this reinforces the truth of choosing to honor and love our partner unconditionally, minimizing future regret and/or resentment.

Standing together as an empowered couple takes work, and a great way to initiate the strength between each other is acknowledging what it is you love about your spouse and loving each other the right way. Sharing what your vision of an empowered couple is and what that looks like for both of you. Feeling and being empowered is about being each other's cheerleader. We get it, sometimes everyday life affects the way we may communicate with our partner.

The little things we say or do to encourage each other can make a world of a difference. A complete game changer for my couples as well as myself has been our "take off and landing"... This is a term used in the "Happy Love" method. Essentially, "take off and landing" is simply making your partner a priority every morning and every evening by simple acts of kindness, such as preparing a cup of coffee or tea for them in the morning and kissing them goodbye.

When your person is off in the world conducting their day, no matter how the day goes, we have set the tone for their arrival home. Let's say there was a minor disagreement that morning and your partner goes storming out and something wonderful happened at work or throughout the day, upon arriving home the recollection of the morning comes to mind. There's a good chance the highlight of the day which might have been shared is now not as significant.

Simon Sniek shares an analogy of believing and committing yourself to the act of kindness on a consistent basis. It's like going to the gym and working out for 9 hours and not seeing any results, as opposed to going to the gym daily for 20 minutes and seeing results over time. This is similar to building empowerment in a relationship. It is not a day of the event, but rather an accumulation of all the little things you do and sacrifices for one another. Yes, there will be obstacles. It is important to remain a united front, not allowing anything to shake your relationship. As time goes on you will become stronger together.

> *"Love recognizes no barriers. It jumps hurdles, leaps fences, penetrates walls to arrive at its destination full of hope"*
> *Maya Angelou*

With courage and commitment, Stephaney Campbell stands behind a wedding industry revolution that brings sustainable practices and perspectives into all weddings and marriages. Stephaney works with couples who wish to foster trust and longevity in your life together, offering coaching and guidance so that your wedding day can be celebrated with comfort and confidence. With her limitless grace and desire to see you grow in your relationship, working with Stephaney feels, for many, as though you've hired your best friend.

ABOUT THE AUTHOR

After nearly a decade of high-caliber executive assistant experience, Stephaney became a certified wedding planner in 2015 and is the owner and lead planner of Inspired Weddings and Events. Modelling her approach to planning on her mother's acute attention to detail and careful organization, Stephaney brings a holistic, sustainable, and curated approach to captivating weddings and extraordinary marriages. With a passion for creating world-class experiences for couples and guests, Stephaney ensures that your celebration is a reflection of your love and intentions for life together.

Whether you seek a sublime destination wedding celebration, dream of hosting a zero-waste event, or wish to customize a commitment ceremony that you and your guests will remember forever, Stephaney is a source of empowerment, supporting you and your partner during this time of transformation.

CONTACT INFORMATION

Stephaney Campbell
Email: hello@inspired-weddings.ca
Website: inspired-weddings.ca
LinkedIn https://www.linkedin.com/in/stephaney-campbell-6b0880b9/

Ean Price Murphy

Dedication

"It's time for you to move, realizing that the thing you are seeking is also seeking you." — *Iyanla Vanzant*

CHAPTER 7

TRANSFORMING YOUR RELATIONSHIP TO MONEY

By Ean Price Murphy

I didn't understand. I thought I had done everything right. I had worked hard, sometimes two and three jobs. I had been as frugal as I could - rarely going out and living with 6 other people in a 4 bedroom apartment. I bought mostly second-hand clothes. And yet.... And yet, I found myself staring at a pile of credit card bills, all maxed out, all overdue, and I couldn't even make the minimum payments. I had to admit it. I was beat. I felt like a failure.

Most of us have some feelings about money: want it, shun it, ignore it, obsess over it. Sometimes we have those feelings in quick succession or even at the same time.

If you know you want more ease and clarity with your relationship to money, you are in the right place.

Growing up, I wasn't given a lot of guidance around money. I was given an allowance and expected to manage my own money from a very young age. I was brought up hearing "work hard and you will succeed" so I imagined that for someone willing to work as hard as I was, success would be easy. Not so much.

I also grew up hearing "follow your passion and the money will come," so I pursued a liberal arts education and balanced theater with bartending and temp work until I began to realize that my bank balance was holding steady near $0 while my credit card, loaded up with groceries and gas purchases, was only growing.

Once I admitted to myself I was in financial trouble, I gave up theater and got a full time job as an office manager … for $9/hour. By that time, I could barely keep up with my minimum payments. Payments that only went towards paying the interest and never touched the principal amount owed. I tried negotiating with the credit companies to lower my rates, I tried opening 0% APR cards and transferring balances. I tried consolidating balances and I tried breaking the balances up. I tried everything I could think of and everything people suggested.

After a year working at the same company, I asked for a raise, since office managers usually made at least $15/hour. But, my boss was also in financial chaos and offered to pay me only $9.25. I was devastated. My financial health was crippled because of someone else's financial instability.

I did the math. and a At that rate of pay, I would make payments for the rest of my life and still not pay off the debt, and live every day with stress, worry and scarcity. What if I needed to go to the dentist? What if I got sick and wasn't able to work for a period of time? What if? What if?

I decided to file for bankruptcy. Integrity is one of my highest values and breaking faith with the companies I owed was incredibly painful - even though they had made their money back from me multiple times. Still, I felt like I had failed. I felt like a failure.

Knowing what I know now, I can give myself grace. I was financially illiterate. I was trying my best without all the information I needed to see the warning signs of financial trouble early enough to do something before it became so terrible, without having all the information I needed. I give myself grace that I didn't yet understand that I might have to change jobs to get paid what I was worth. I didn't yet understand that the vast majority of small businesses operate check to check, in debt, and in financial chaos just like the people who run them.

Fortunately, I had picked up bookkeeping skills in my role as an office manager. So, I decided to strike out on my own as a freelancer and charge $25 an hour. I was determined to transform my financial life. I resolved *never* to go into credit card debt again and to learn exactly what I had to to make sure I avoided it. And I have kept that resolution for 30 years and counting now.

A key element that supported this huge change in my life goes beyond simply avoiding debt. As an experience, living through a bankruptcy transformed my relationship with money. It Ttransformed it by changing how I thought about money and how I thought about the world and myself.

I had always thought of money as a necessary evil, a unit of exchange in which I begrudgingly gave up my time so that I could pay my bills. When I started working for myself, I could set my price based on what I wanted to charge to have a comfortable life - not just what a boss was able to afford to pay me. When I was able to charge based on the value I provided and find clients who wanted the services I was offering, my relationship to money transformed. The daily stress and worry dissipated and I found that most months I had a little extra money to do with as I wished. Conversations with myself about my goals and values and how I wanted to save or use the excess became normal. I was able to put money away for retirement, save for vacations, and support charities that were important to me. I came to realize is thatrealize that money is necessary to be able to catalyze the changes I wanted to see in my life, my community, and the world. Now I no longer view money as a unit of exchange for time, but for impact. I no longer view money as neutral but as a tool for good.

I also learned that it is t n't simply a matter of "making more". After the basic needs are covered, there is a strategy and an intention about how to organize, save, spend, and invest the money you have in order to build a strong and sustainable business that supports the owner, the staff, and the community.

Now I make it my mission to help radically kind entrepreneurs get comfortable with money so they can focus on impact, not spreadsheets or financial worry.

Here are my top tips on transforming your relationship with money, whatever it may be, so that money serves your highest purpose.

1. **Determine your life values**

Once you know what is most important to you, it is easier to reduce or eliminate all the distractions of unimportant things. And making financial decisions based on what isn't actually important to us can really lead us down the wrong path. That's when we get a job we hate so we can afford something we don't want. Or when we spend money on clothing to fit in when we'd rather travel or buy all the craft materials.

So, sit down and ask yourself some questions. If being creative is what gives you life, how much would it take to make you feel ok about having that time taken from you? If stability is important to you, what sorts of things would make you feel that most deeply? What are your values? There are so many values lists around to sit down with and select from. Find your north star, and focus on that.

2. **Let go of standards and worrying about what other people think**

One of the stumbling blocks to focusing on what matters most to you is worrying what others are doing, thinking, or buying. Watching the journey of others, or listening too closely to conventional wisdom, can keep you stuck for years.

In order to let a new way of relating to money emerge, you may have to let go of other ways of being, whether it be the "starving artist" or "stylish host" or saying yes to those store brand credit cards. You don't have to do anything to prove your worth to others, or respond to what they want from you. Instead, relentlessly pursue proving your worthiness to yourself, and follow your own inner voice to what really matters to you, your values, your perspective, your gifts.

3. **Practice grace and gratitude**

You may have some financial missteps in your past. You are not alone, and you never have to try and be perfect. There is no such thing. So give yourself grace. And remember all you have to be grateful for. Being kind to yourself, and thankful towards life is a super power combo.

I make a daily habit of taking the first few moments of the day to deeply appreciate the things I have, and a few minutes at the end of every day to recognize the things I did well, even if the outcomes are not yet what I want.

4. **Get comfortable with your fears and your discomfort**

This is a big one, and kinda at the foundation of all growth. Most people are held back by fears of some kind, often fear of shame or others' judgements, or of just feeling plain awful. If worrying about looking foolish or wanting to never make a mistake are is holding you back, you can begin by expanding your capacity to experience these things. Start practicing public silliness in small ways to see that you can be foolish, be judged or laughed at, and still - magically - be OK. You'll be building up tolerance and strength in yourself. Not to mention, mistakes are how we learn. As in, only by making mistakes is there an opportunity to learn. No mistakes, no growth. Celebrate the things that went wrong - apologize when appropriate but also celebrate the beautiful mess of being a human. And get used to moving ahead despite your fears or discomfort. Whatever you want is on the other side of those feelings.

> *"As in, only by making mistakes is there an opportunity to learn. No mistakes, no growth."*

5. **Get help with money mindset**

This tip is a two part-er! First, get help, find a community, enroll enlist support. It's hard to teach yourself something you don't know. There are some things you can eventually figure out, but why not give others the gift of sharing what they know with you? A supportive community is a truly powerful tool.

Next, devote some time and energy to learning how to shift your mindset, and specifically your habitual (and possibly unhelpful) thoughts about money.

There is so much new information about how brains work and how to change your brain and your habits, go find it and start implementing, just one change at a time.

Transformation requires evaluation, organization, and implementation. Know why you want to change, what you will change, and how you will change it - and then get the support you need to take the next right action.

So, what is your next right action? What one thing will you do RIGHT NOW to begin the financial transformation journey?

ABOUT THE AUTHOR

Ean Price Murphy, the founder of Moxie Bookkeeping and Coaching Inc, teaches successful heart-driven entrepreneurs a dead-simple cash management system that works with their natural habits so they don't have to learn accounting to become permanently profitable and can focus on impact not spreadsheets.

Ean is a certified Mastery level Profit First Professional, Xero Platinum partner, Quickbooks ProAdvisor, and a certified business coach.

CONTACT INFORMATION

Ean Price Murphy
Moxie Bookkeeping & Coaching Inc
ean@moxiebookkeeping.com
https://www.linkedin.com/in/eanpricemurphy/
www.moxiebookkeeping.com

> *"Yes, your transformation will be hard. Yes, you will feel frightened, messed up and knocked down. Yes, you'll want to stop. Yes, it's the best work you'll ever do."*
> *Robin Sharma*

Elisa Magill

Dedication

This chapter is dedicated to all those countless amazing people who have motivated and inspired me throughout the years. Those people who – despite all their challenges, setbacks, and doubts – rose above it all to stay energized to endure their trials and thrive, reaching true transformational success in the process! Observing all of you has truly inspired me... showing that if you stick with your dream, anything is possible. For that, I thank you!!!

CHAPTER 8

THE ENERGY TRANSFORMATION EQUATION

HARNESS YOUR ENERGY TO TRANSFORM YOUR IDEAS INTO REALITY TODAY

By Elisa Magill, MBA, M.S., Ph.D.

*"Energy cannot be created or destroyed,
it can only be changed from
one form to another."*
~ Albert Einstein

Daniel was on top of the world...he had a great business idea and was successfully transforming his dreams into reality. Business was growing and his future looked promising! However, something unexpected happened. A pandemic swept the world and changed everything. His plans were for a societal system that was no longer functioning as expected. People weren't buying as they had before, no one was meeting in person anymore or leaving their homes unless they had to. Businesses were shutting down. Daniel did not know what to do as he watched his bank account dwindle to nothing. One day he woke up and realized that he had two choices. He could stand up and get moving again, or he could stay where he was, shutting down, and give up. The latter was not an option. He decided to stand up and push forward toward his goal, to make his dreams a reality despite the setbacks, despite the naysayers, despite the grim outlook. As he started his journey toward recovery he wondered, "what am I doing and why?!?" Instead of discouraging him, the final word in this self-imposed question inspired him. He started to think about his "why" and realized that his desire to transform his life would guide him to the life of his dreams. He realized that he could do more, help more, reach more, and be more once he attained his goal. He decided that the pain of not achieving his goal would be worse than the pain it would take to get back up and rebuild his momentum. So... instead of shutting down, he took back control of his life and made it happen...he pushed through everything, endured the chaos, and turned his dreams into reality. By building momentum and energy toward his vision, he transformed his life!

"He realized that he could do more, help more, reach more, and be more once he attained his goal. He decided that the pain of not achieving his goal would be worse than the pain it would take to get back up and rebuild his momentum."

Although the above story is hypothetical, this unfortunately was a reality for many business owners during the 2020 Covid-19 pandemic with their existing business models. It wasn't uncommon to hear about a new entrepreneurial venture that shut down, or a mom-and-pop store that had to close its doors. For some, they had no choice as there were no more options to attain the cash they needed; however, for others it was the will to continue that was the challenge.

Although there is enough material on this topic to warrant its own book, for this particular chapter, we will be focusing more on the will to push forward… or the motivation to continue when the going gets tough. After a major setback or discouragement, how can you find the motivation, or the energy, to move at all? Then, how do you create momentum strong enough to lead to true transformational success? The following sections will discuss three simple steps (the energy transformation equation) you can take to rebuild your energy and point you in the direction leading to transformation: Momentum + Energy = Endurance (M+E = E). We will examine each factor of the equation below.

MOMENTUM

What is momentum? It is the force that grows and builds to push you forward at a consistent pace in the direction of your goal. It is energy that flows stronger and stronger in a targeted direction with purpose. To illustrate, think of an ocean wave. Far out at sea, it may be a slow-moving current. Then, it gets closer to shore, and that current suddenly gains momentum, enough to crescendo down to the ocean floor, continuing forward until it spreads out as it reaches the shore. That final push is momentum. What about a young child roller skating? When they learn, they may not put that much energy into their skating. They may be hesitant and may not push their legs too far in fear of going too fast. However, as they become used to the feeling of the skates, they begin to put more energy into their movements to go faster. Then, they may become more adventurous, skating down steep hills and racing their friends. This intentional forward movement, which picks up speed as it goes, is also momentum. It is something that becomes very difficult (or impossible) to stop when it becomes strong. For example... try stopping a tsunami. It probably won't happen.

Why am I sharing these examples with you? It is important for you to visualize the true meaning of momentum. It's not just moving forward; it is making sure you do it in such a way that each movement makes it more impossible for you to stop. It will make continued and more impactful movement more probable. It will make progression easier. It is where the energy flow is intentional and directed. This is what we want when it comes to our business... intentional energy flows!

ENERGY

Let's focus a bit on energy. As Albert Einstein's quote at the beginning of this chapter suggests, energy does not disappear, it merely changes forms. For example, gasoline (or electricity for some cars) changes into energy that propels (or builds momentum) in an automobile. Food changes into energy for living creatures. Sunshine triggers the production of Vitamin D in our bodies. Oxygen is considered the "breath of life," energizing our bodies to pump blood, which feeds our body's cells, without which we would not have any energy to live. So yes, we all have energy, or we would not be living...it's just that some have more energy than others, or are more skilled at harnessing that energy toward achieving their desired results.

Unfortunately, in the world we live in, there are energy thieves. Things that create, overwhelm and burnout in our daily lives, both personally and professionally. Being able to identify these will help us to better manage our energy and to save our energy from "energy vampires" (negative situations that drain all the energy out of our souls), or to harness our energy (find positive situations that recharge our battersbatteries and inspire/motivate us). Some call this "resiliency," or endurance.

ENDURANCE

As stated above, resiliency is a close relative to endurance. As resilience is the "bounce back" factor, meaning you are skilled at being able to get back up after being kicked down (like Daniel was in the opening example) then you would be defined as resilient. Resiliency is the main ingredient for one to endure.

However, more is required when it comes to endurance. To endure hardship, the proactive individual would first identify, and then look to acquire the skills and abilities he or she may need to be successful in their stated endeavors. They would also learn enough about themselves as an individual to identify what it is that either drains or fuels their personal energy for sustained results. They would look to not just learn and acquire these new skills and/or insights, but they would look to apply these to their personal and/or professional lives in a way that would create transformative change… moving from one state of being to another by applying what was learned. We would filter incoming information through our personal perceptions to create meaning (Mezirow, 1997). In this way, the transformation could be said to be successful as the individual achieved what they set out to accomplish. They did not give up.

CREATING YOUR REALITY

"Everything is energy & that's all there is to it. Match the frequency of the reality you want and you cannot help but get that reality. It can be no other way. This is not philosophy. This is physics." ~ Darryl Anka

Today, self-help books are abundant and available to us from multiple sources. Many of these books discuss the potential to create our own realities. Is it "fluff?" Is it something a "con-artist" came up with to steal millions from those who wish it to be true? Some would say this is the case. However, the research shows that there is something to the belief we share in a cause. In a sense, when we think something and believe it to be true, we are energizing that belief. We are giving it life. When we continue to envision that reality, our brain will believe it to be true, and will work to make that belief a reality (Hill, 2008).

This is why some research will show that visualization works. If the brain thinks negativenegatively, negative thoughts and actions will follow. However, if our brain envisions positive outcomes, our thoughts and actions will follow in that desired direction. In this way, we can build momentum and energy in any direction we choose. This is why it is so important to pay attention to what we are reading, watching, talking about, envisioning, and saying to ourselves! The brain does not know the difference between what is real and what is not real... it believes what it hears. In fact, when we visualize, vocalize, and write down that in which we desire to manifest, chances are we will bring those dreams to reality (Hill, 2008). What we tell ourselves, whether positive or negative, will affect our intentionality and subsequent actions (Berger & Tobar, 2019). So be mindful of your self-talk!

However, knowing this, the individual has a much better chance of first envisioning, then outlining in detail the future reality they desire. Once this vision is identified, a strategy to attain it needs to be set, and a realistic plan of action created. This is the Vision + Strategy + Action (VSA) formula. In a sense, this is how the individual can direct and harness their energy. Otherwise, it will be scattered. Think about someone who loves to cook, but they walk into a kitchen that has several pots and several sets of ingredients. If they are not familiar with the kitchen or are not a skilled chef, they may not know where to begin. They know they need to produce an entire meal, but they look around... start to feel overwhelmed, and then freeze. Or, instead of freezing, they are scattered... running around the kitchen trying to prepare all the meals at once, but not feeling effective in preparing any of them. Business is similar.

There is always so much to do and so many directions we could go. We might have what it takes to become successful (all the ingredients), and we may have the knowledge (experience cooking), but we might not know the goals and/or what to do first since we just walked into a full kitchen with ingredients and utensils everywhere. First, we need to know what we are supposed to make (our short and long-term goals). Then, we'll know which dish to start making first (or which steps to work on first in our business). Then, we'll be able to prioritize our plans and actions in a targeted direction with the intent to reach envisioned and strategizedstrategic goals. This is how we create momentum and energy in our business.

How do we incorporate endurance into this? Well, using the above analogy of cooking, let's say you finished cooking the meal, but it won't be served until the next day,. wWhat do you do? You wrap it all up and seal it well and refrigerate it. That will preserve it as fresh until it's time to be served. Endurance is much the same. It is what we need to do to keep everything we've worked hard to create alive and well. Instead of throwing the food or our hard work away, we know how to take care of it and ourselves so that we can withstand the test of time. This is why it's also important to know ourselves and what activities we need to do to stay energized for the long haul. It can be tempting to just keep running toward our goals in the hopes of getting there faster without pausing to recharge our batteries. Remember the common saying, "maturity is the ability to postpone gratification?" In the world we live in, we need to exhibit these traits more so than ever.

CONCLUSION

Just as knowing the purpose of making a meal (who is it for, type of dishes expected, timeline meals are expected to be finished…eaten…stored, etc.) in order to be effective in your actions and to avoid feeling scattered and misdirected, we need to know these things about our business as well. Without a crystal-clear vision, an intentional and well thought out strategy and action plan, we will feel distracted, overwhelmed, and frustrated. If unchecked, this can lead to a pretty significant case of burnout.

Therefore, it is important to put time into the VSA equation and especially your M+E = E equation. Without these elements – vision, strategy, and action; and momentum, energy, and endurance – your career dreams may stay just that... something you like to think about now and then. Or something you'll recognize that others have from time to time and simply wish for. Instead, if you work hard to solidify these elements and you know the exact direction you want to go in, you will stay motivated... building momentum and energy to incorporate the steps you need to produce endurance. You will get there! You will not be the one looking from the outside in. You will not be sitting in a chair at the end of your years wondering, "what if?" Instead, you will be sitting in your chair, proudly looking at the pictures that captured this extraordinary life you created. You'll be reading the stories of those you helped, of the lives you changed for the better. Instead of "what if," you'll be saying "what if I didn't...thank goodness I harnessed my energy and transformed my ideas into this amazing reality I am reflecting upon today!" And...d this, my friends..., is when true transformational success makes history.

REFERENCES

Berger, B. G., & Tobar, D. A. (2019). Moving away from counterproductive thoughts in

Exercise settings: Perfectionism, self-talk, self-handicapping, and social loafing.

In APA handbook of sport and exercise psychology, volume 2: Exercise psychology.

Vol. 2. (pp. 387–407). American Psychological Association.

https://doi.org/10.1037/0000124-020

Hill, N. (2008). Think and grow rick: the complete classic text – Delux ed. New York, NY:

   Penguin Random House

Mezirow, J. (Summer 1997). NEW DIRECTIONS FOR ADULT AND CONTINUING

   EDUCATION, no. 74, Jossey-Bass Publishers.

ABOUT THE AUTHOR

Dr. Elisa Magill is the CEO of Endurance Business Builders and the Academy for Transformational Success, specializing in harnessing ones' personal energy, performance improvement, distraction management, and creating a business that endures the test of time while avoiding burnout. Elisa combines her Ph.D. in Industrial/Organizational Psychology, and MBA in Executive Management and Entrepreneurship with her decades of applied experience centered around emotional intelligence and resiliency research to support and empower her clients to ignite their dreams and "Make it Happen Now!" Elisa is the Amazon bestselling author of "Harness Your Entrepreneurial ADD: How to Move from Distraction to Action in the Age of Information Overload to Supercharge Your Profits." She is continually dedicated to discovering new ways to help people reach their true potential… creating success by design versus default!

CONTACT INFORMATION

Elisa Magill, MBA, Ph.D.
Endurance Business Builders

CEO, Brain Energy & Performance Expert
Endurance for Business, Endurance for Life!
(951) 426-0688
www.ElisaMagill.com
www.Linkedin.com/in/ElisaMagill

*Imperfections are not inadequacies; they
are reminders that we're all in this together.
Brene Brown*

Gina Marie De Leon

Dedication

Thank you to my extraordinary mentors for sharing of your expertise, showing me the right path, and illuminating my mind. You have left a a footprint on my life never to be forgotten.

CHAPTER 9

SHOULD I STAY OR SHOULD I GO?

By Gina Marie De Leon

"When you experience uncertainty, you are on the right path, so don't give up"
Deepak Chopra

Having worked with hundreds of direct sellers in all stages of personal and business development, I am convinced that people begin a transformation as they transition from being an employee to becoming an entrepreneur, and struggle through the question, should I stay, or should I go? Is it the right time to change companies or start my own business?

I have a lot of people that will reach out to me privately with this question and I am going to just let you know up front I do not give advice either way. It is a personal decision that each of us will live with it one way or the other, good or bad. I can offer a perspective on things to think about and consider, most of which is the reason you are thinking of leaving and is an important conversation to be had before taking the leap. Even if you are not considering going, I promise you this will be a valuable chapter because, at some point in your career, you may have someone on your team that is having this thought and you will be able to have a leadership conversation with them that might make a difference in helping them make the right choice.

First, know that it is all right if you decide at some point in your career that the company you are with now may not be the right fit moving forward. I do not have the actual figures, but I can tell you many of the people that are successful in this profession did not do it with their first company. They have gone through several companies on their journey to success within the direct sales industry, and I am one of them.

The first question I want you to ask yourself is why you are considering leaving? Is it because the company is no longer aligned with the things that you are passionate about? Have you tried a product that has transformed your life and you just want to have your personal story serve as the foundation for building your business? Is there something with the company that you are concerned about? Sometimes things fundamentally change, whether it is within you or the way the company is operating. These are legitimate reasons why you may consider going somewhere else, but here is the only piece of advice I will give you in this area; make the decision and do not waver back and forth. Too many times I see people trying to build teams with two different companies, their train of thought is 'I'm going to build company B on the side while continuing to work with company A until I can replace my current income.' You may not see it yet, but at some point you will have to choose, it is hard enough to build one business, much less two. Most people that are doing this is because they are not really that financially successful in company A and they think that the grass is greener in Company B, and do not want to make the wrong decision. That is the wrong way of looking at it, it is not about making the right decision, it is about deciding and then committing to making that decision right.

Whether you stay or go, make the decision and plant your flag, because the people that have made an impact and have become financially successful in this business are those that stood the test of time. It is all right if you want to go somewhere else, but do not be a company hopper the minute things get tough or you are never going to have staying power in this profession. The people that have staying power are the ones that find a company that they are aligned with in terms of their values, they believe the leadership has character and integrity, they love the products, and it is a fair compensation plan. They plant their flag in the ground and they get to work, ride the ups and downs, they understand there are good years and bad years, but they never waver. They have a vision, and they keep going, and that is why they succeed.

Often, I see people moving companies and running into the exact same reasons they initially decided to move because they never addressed the underlying issue, which is their lack of belief. Be honest with yourself in this area. Have you given the company a fair try and focused on all the right things? What specifically needs to change for it to work, and do you have reasonable grounds on which to believe that is likely to happen and in what time frame? Do you believe that another company is more aligned with your vision, are you passionate about it and believe it is a better place for you? If you choose to leave do not second guess yourself. Leave with integrity, do not try to come back and recruit people from your previous downline. They are going to find out that you are leaving and if you operate from a place of leading with integrity you are going to win in the end. Remember, this is a personal choice, it may not be the right company for you, but do not take away their opportunity to choose what is best for them.

There are lots of layers and a lot of factors which can feel like an impossible decision to make. Even if we feel we have the answer, following through and pulling the trigger can feel incredibly challenging and overwhelming. If you are in that place of feeling overwhelmed, honor the feelings that come with gaining clarity, making sure that you are distilling down what happened into lessons and learning so you know your past struggles were not in vain. Figure out what the future looks like, and who you want to be? What kind of values do you want to bring into your next business? Honor the past while looking to the future. Once you are clear on your expectations it is less daunting to make the choice to stay or walk away. I am clear on my expectations for my continued loyal service within a company, which are salary commensurate to responsibilities, promotion based on results, and continued personal growth. If these expectations have not been met within a reasonable time frame, I begin to seek new opportunities. These expectations should not be taken as a sense of entitlement, but be aware of your worth within the company due to the time, effort, and successful results given.

Taking a leap of faith

> *"In actual life every great enterprise begins with and takes its first forward step in faith"*
> *-- August Von Schlegel*

Once you have taken a deep introspection and have a clear vision of what your future looks like, you may decide that moving on to another company is the way to go. It can be for another established company, or you can decide to establish your own business. After a decade of leading successful direct sellers through their own entrepreneurial journey, I realized most of my time was spent helping them develop emotional stamina, learning how to be courageous, making necessary changes and overcoming the obstacles that were holding them back. I became aware that personal growth, while secondary in their minds, became their primary accomplishment, and guiding network marketers through this emotional labyrinth became my calling. I nurtured and guided them while they felt joy, fear, trust, anger, exhaustion, and every emotion in between. As they worked through those emotions, their business grew, and their transformation began.

I realized that anyone could decide to be an entrepreneur. As one reaches a level of personal wholeness and growth, this yearning for an expression of oneself comes forth. This transition to entrepreneurship exists whether one is in the idea phase, still has a job while starting a business, or is running a business full-time. For me it was the latter, as I worked full time in supporting other leaders, I enrolled in several training courses to feed my passion for learning, allowing me to share with my team in order to support their successes and mine. As I nurtured my personal growth it became clear that my values were no longer aligned with my upline and when the decision to part ways came about, I was ready to embrace becoming my own boss. A terrifying thought for a single mom whose son is about to go off to college. I felt vulnerable and exposed. Thankfully my strong Christian faith, my family's love, and mentorship from my business colleagues kept me in a positive mindset and gave me the courage to move forward and not waver. I acknowledged my desire and became willing to move through the experience, realizing that anything was possible with determination, and belief.

> *"Go confidently in the direction*
> *of your dreams!*
> *Live the life you have imagined."*
> *Henry David Thoreau.*

You have worked through the first emotional challenge of becoming an entrepreneur, you asked the tough questions, and made the decision to leave what you know, be it the security of a job a career or a paycheck; you have embraced courage and are willingly stepping out into the unknown. Bravery and courage are learned behaviors which you will invoke on a regular basis while transforming into a successful entrepreneur.

Whether you decide to stay or walk away, it is not an easy decision to make and not one to take lightly. If you're in that place I'm sending a lot of love to you because I've been there and I know that it's hard, even if you know for some time what you want, it can take a long time to be ready, and no one can force you to get there quicker than you are ready to get there. Please be gentle and compassionate with yourself, do not listen to your inner critical voices of self-judgment and self-criticism telling you are doing something wrong. It is a tough, messy, and complicated decision to make and there is no wrong answer, so give yourself a lot of grace.

REFERENCES

1. Johnson, Omar. "How to Transform Yourself from Employee to Online Entrepreneur"

2. Your Virtual Upline by Bob Heilig

ABOUT THE AUTHOR

Gina Marie De Leon, Founder of Direct Sales Blueprint, with over 10 years of field experience as a bi-lingual English and Spanish Direct Selling Leader, Trainer, and Coach. She is a proud partner of Powerful Women Today as a Mentor Expert, where she continues her love to teach and learn together as a tribe. Her passion for learning continues while pursuing her Certification as a Direct Sales Coach with Direct Sales World Alliance, and her ACC Coaching certification with ICF (International Coaching Federation).

She is passionate about an industry that opens the doors for culturally diverse women from different socioeconomic, and educational backgrounds to become entrepreneurs. Her guiding compasses are God and Family.

It is my mission to empower multi-tasking women to accomplish greatness and reach new heights within this amazing industry. Guide them through the pitfalls of working from home to successfully integrate both their home and business lives to achieve success.

If you are new to Direct Sales or have been idling for a while in your home business, and are ready to scale up, and experience a flexible business lifestyle, let's connect on LinkedIn:

#OwnYourBusiness #OwnYourLife

CONTACT INFORMATION

Gina Marie De Leon
https://www.linkedin.com/in/direct-sales-blueprint-12223-gina-marie

If you take care of your mind, you take care of the world.
Arianna Huffington

Melanie Herschorn

Dedication

To my Dad, Sender, who supports me unconditionally and paved the way to my successes.

CHAPTER 10

HOW TO BECOME A SUBJECT MATTER EXPERT

By Melanie Herschorn

I never wanted to be a doctor.

As a small child, I watched firsthand what it was like to be a successful physician. It meant waking up at 6 am, seeing patients instead of eating lunch, getting home late at night only to ignore your children, scarfing down dinner, and doing paperwork until the wee hours. Then repeat. Weekends weren't for family time and if you got a call in the middle of the night, no matter how exhausted you were, you had to go and work until you were done.

Tired? Drink more coffee.

Missed your kid's school play? Patients come first.

Have plans? Forget them and do your duty when an emergency arises.

None of that appealed to me at all. I've always gravitated toward creative endeavors. While I don't need a lot of sleep, I do need my alone time. And if someone tried dictating my schedule to me, I would be rather miserable.

I did not take more than the bare minimum of science classes in high school. There was no way I was going to live that kind of life.

However, this lack of interest in medicine presented a problem for me. My entire family is in the medical field. There was therefore an expectation that I, too, would become a "professional".

When I heard that, I remember thinking, "Does that mean anyone who is not a doctor, lawyer, or engineer by default is not a professional?"

I wondered if it made these "nonprofessionals" less than. I also wondered if it meant that as a "non-professional" I would never be able to make a lot of money. But given how awful that life sounded, I hedged my bets against joining it.

Do you know what they call the person who graduates at the bottom of their medical school class? Doctor.

Even that person is considered a subject matter expert. They know medicine. You defer to them and never call them Ms. or Mr. So, stuck in that line of thinking, I ventured into adulthood under the assumption that I would never be an expert in anything that mattered.

My Path to becoming a Professional

In college, I studied history, which was kind of professional, but when I learned that those who go on to a Ph.D. often develop lung issues after spending time with old, decrepit books, I bowed out of going further. I fell into Public Relations after graduation and learned as I went. It wasn't considered "professional" by my family's standards because I was working with celebrities, but I enjoyed it nonetheless. Within just a few years though, I was frustrated with some of the aspects of working with stars and I wanted more.

When I spoke to my family about my desire to leave, they highly endorsed that. They reminded me of the time a celebrity client handed me their gum prior to walking on stage for a TV show taping. I should definitely get out of that line of work. No professional would ever be asked to take gum from another human.

Ever the people pleaser, I moved into journalism. That's professional, I thought. My family approves, I thought. I busted my ass and got a master's degree and even finished top of my class.

By age 32, I was still waiting to feel like a subject matter expert in anything, though. I had almost felt like one in public relations but then I left to pursue a more "professional" career. Six years after getting that degree, I'd been a radio news anchor and reporter for a while, but with the vast array of stories I covered, I never felt like an expert in any particular subject.

Then I got laid off when I was pregnant, and I was back to square one. Ever the optimist, I still believed that I would find my path of professional expertise. This time, however, I pursued a completely different occupation. I'd recently had a baby and saw an opportunity. As a kid, I'd secretly wanted to be a fashion designer, but never even entertained the idea seriously (it's not a professional path, wink wink) but this would be my chance: Women needed fashionable and functional nursing wear and I could fill that void. Plus, being an entrepreneur is professional-ish, right?

By year seven of the business, I was selling my clothes on Nordstrom.com, Amazon, and in boutiques across North America. My products had won awards and the business was making money. But still feeling like a non-expert, I hired a marketing person to help me. That was unfortunately the beginning of the end of the business. I paid her lots of money to do my marketing and teach me along the way, but she belittled me and my abilities to the point where I had no self-esteem or marketing budget left.

The Breakthrough

It was only then, when I felt like a shell of a person, that things became so clear. I'm thrilled to be able to share my discovery with you:

Transforming into the expert you want to be is not about spending 10,000 hours to hone your craft, a number that's been attributed to author Malcolm Gladwell. You don't even have to be a "professional" (whatever the heck that means).

What you really need to have is the right mindset and a few tools in your arsenal that I've outlined below.

Yes. It can be that uncomplicated. It can even be done without attending medical school.

I know a lot of experts who are too encumbered by imposter syndrome to charge for their expertise. I used to be (and sometimes still am) one of them. Even my dog sitter has trouble asking for her desired fee after 28 years in the business.

The first time I ever charged someone for marketing services, I was so terribly nervous. But I talked myself through it. I knew that I could help her with email marketing because I'd been doing it effectively for years. When she asked what it would cost, I held my breath and practically whispered "$100." The two seconds it took her to answer felt like an eternity. But her response was swift. "Sure. Is PayPal, ok?"

I no longer charge $100 for services, but I'm not yet at the point like Supermodel Linda Evangelista who said "I don't get out of bed for less than $10,000 a day." The point is, you may not feel like you know enough or even that you are enough. But let me tell you something...you do, and you are.

As I was writing this chapter, recalling my varied work experiences, I realized that each of those times, I *kind of* was a subject matter expert by the end. Remember when I said that I was a general assignment reporter so I couldn't have known enough about any one subject? Well, the truth is, I won several prestigious journalism awards during my tenure, I learned the geography of a state that I couldn't find on a map prior to living there, I memorized names and facts about dozens of ongoing stories and even more information about local politicians during that time. I can guarantee that I knew more about Pennsylvania than practically anyone in Seattle.

But at the time, and even several paragraphs ago, I couldn't see it. It's hard to get that perspective when you're too close.

I'd like you to take a moment right now and make a list of three things that you know about your industry like the back of your hand. I bet you will find that you're a subject matter expert already. And if you're in doubt, here are three tools to have in your toolbox that will help you step into your rightful place as an SME (subject matter expert).

Expert Tool No. 1

Continue learning. I don't mean that you have to go back to school and get a doctorate if that doesn't make sense for your line of work. I decided to go back to school because I didn't think I knew enough yet to be a good journalist by simply learning on the job. While I knew a lot more heading into my first journalism job because of my schooling, there was still an incredibly steep learning curve. I had never actually gone live on the radio or written a news story for radio. I'd never been on a real deadline.

I had to keep learning as I went. And I continue to do so. Trends change. Technology changes. People change. I certainly can't market to Baby boomers and Gen Z-ers the same way, so I need to be well-educated about my target audience and how to appeal to them best. Don't get stuck in the past. There's always something new to add to your arsenal to help you step into expert status.

Expert Tool No. 2

Teach what you do know. Now you may stop me and say, Wait! If you want me to continue learning new things, how can I also teach? Let me tell it to you straight. You'll never know everything. A lot of entrepreneurs get caught in this endless loop of buying courses and never implementing what they learn because they feel like they don't know enough yet. Do not let that be you. As you learn, begin to teach others what you know.

You can be a guest on a podcast, speak at an online summit, or create a new course. The people who are a year behind you in business will benefit from your instruction. Even if other people do what you do, they won't do it exactly the way you do. As you begin to teach more, those around you will view you as an expert in that area.

Expert Tool No. 3

Write a book and market it to your ideal clients and customers. Sound a bit daunting? It doesn't have to be. There are so many opportunities for you to write a book in a way that fits your lifestyle and schedule.

Book coaches and author coaches can help guide you through the writing process. Developmental editors help with piecing together the content in a coherent and cohesive way. Line editors make it grammatically correct. Some book coaches specialize in helping you take your blog posts and turn them into a book. Others show you how to write a book in 30 days, 90 days, or longer. You can join a multi-author book like the one you're reading right now (so meta, right?!). If you don't want to write at all, you can hire a ghostwriter to do the heavy lifting for you.

Publishing is so much easier than ever before. You are no longer reliant on a traditional publisher to choose you from a sea of would-be authors. Hybrid publishers help you publish your book to make it available online in ALL the places. You also have the option to self-publish, meaning you can do it all yourself. There's no longer a barrier to entry.

As you craft and begin to execute a book marketing strategy, you'll begin to grow your audience, sell books, fill your programs with excited clients, and be asked to speak on podcasts and on stages. That book and its marketing will be important devices to help you call yourself (and really feel like) a subject matter expert.

Feelings Matter

The "feeling" part is important to touch upon. Many of us are our own worst enemies. We can get all the positive feedback in the world but if we hear one negative comment, we'll fixate on it. If one person says something that triggers us to make us question our expertise, we're likely to wonder if we should just throw in the towel now.

Whenever this happens, I want you to go back to tools 1 through 3. Read something to make you feel like you've gained some new knowledge. Share that knowledge with someone you can help. Then, consider writing about your expertise in a book so that you can support even more people across the globe. With a book and a plan to market it, the sky is the limit.

ABOUT THE AUTHOR

Melanie Herschorn wants to make your book and brand sparkle online. As a content marketing strategist for coaches, consultants, and speakers worldwide, she's on a mission to support and empower her clients to create clear messaging and content that shines a light on their individuality, skillset, and books.

With her unique combination of entrepreneurship, award-winning journalism and PR experience, Melanie guides her clients to attract and nurture leads and position themselves as industry experts. She also loves to give book marketing tips on her live show Authority Marketing Live!

CONTACT INFORMATION

Melanie Herschorn
Book Marketing Strategist & Coach
https://www.linkedin.com/in/melanie-herschorn-a8122126/
https://www.facebook.com/groups/vipdigitalmarketingtips/
vipdigitalcontent.com
melanie@vipdigitalcontent.com

"At fifty-four, I am still in progress, and I hope that I always will be."
Michelle Obama

Mindy McManus

Dedication

I would like to dedicate this chapter to my amazing husband Jimi McManus. Jimi has supported me on my transformation journey and I have seen him transform in many ways since we've been together. We both encourage and support each other when transformation is upon us. Thank you for loving me, Jimi, and making me your wife. I look forward to how we transform together and reach our dreams and goals in our marriage and professional lives.

CHAPTER 11

TAPPING INTO THE POWER OF TRANSFORMATION

TURNING YOUR MESS INTO YOUR MESSAGE

By Mindy McManus

The darkest four years in my life was two years after an emergency appendectomy in Cozumel Mexico and just before COVID happened. I was on my first cruise with my ex-husband and the vacation was not going well. His mental illness had gotten to a point where he was unable to manage his behavior. I remember thinking to myself that this was it. After the cruise I was planning on leaving him. Then, hurricane Irma was headed towards Miami Florida and many of the cruise's passengers needed to get back to Miami to board up their homes and we were offered the options of getting off the cruise or staying on, not knowing when or where we'd land. Our truck didn't have any gas and was parked on one of the top levels of the parking garage.

We knew we'd be stuck in traffic from the Florida Keys evacuating, and there were many reports of gas stations running out of gas. We decided to stay on the cruise. The cruise left Miami again on Thursday with Irma on its way to South Florida, another hurricane called Maria was headed towards northern Mexico. It was that Thursday night when I got sick. Really sick. So sick that I had to go to the emergency department on the ship. I was in so much pain. The emergency department wasn't able to determine what was going on, but they thought that it was my appendix. At that time, my ex-husband was very upset and was very adamant that he did not want to get off the cruise for me to get to a hospital. He told me to not show that I was in pain when the cruise doctor would press down on my lower abdomen. I remember my ex-husband yelling "we are not getting off this boat, you are not having surgery in a foreign country". Saturday morning rolled around, and I hadn't had any sleep and the only TV station that was in English was the weather channel. Pain medicine keeps me awake so I was in a cruise bed, watching Hurricane Irma and Maria on the weather channel, and feeling emotionally unsafe.

Saturday at 8am the ship docked in Cozumel Mexico. The stretcher from the ambulance was outside the hospital emergency department at 8:03. I was at the hospital by 8:15am and they rushed me to get a CT scan after we gave them our credit card, which they then proceeded to put $2,000 on in order to see me. Next thing I know, the surgeon came into my emergency room and told me that I needed emergency surgery and that they are prepping the surgical room. I then remembered that I could be life-flighted out of there with the benefits that my company offered. I was told that if I waited any longer to have surgery that I was going to die. My appendix was perforated and was leaking into my gut for days. I was septic and was going to die. My life flashed before my eyes, and then I had a sense of calm come over me. I realized that I had met my dreams and goals for my life, and I felt complete. I was ready to go to heaven if that was my fate that day.

My fate was not to die that day, even though it took me a few more days to clear the infection. Thankfully, we had travel insurance, and they took care of getting us home.

The next two years were dark. They were the two years leading up to the pandemic. I decided to give my husband another chance since he stepped up after the surgery and took care of me. However, once I was ok, he went back into his selfish and needy ways.

When the pandemic hit, I had just left my husband, living on my own with my two dogs, one a puppy. My full time job at a healthcare company had just furloughed a majority of their non-clinician employees. I was devastated and didn't know what to do and didn't know how I was going to pay my bills. I remember writing on LinkedIn that there would be a reckoning for leaders and organizations who didn't care for their employees during the pandemic, who treated their people like garbage and fired many people. Now, organizations can't find good help. The people have spoken, and they are not willing to work for a leader or an organization that doesn't put the needs of their employees in their top three priorities. The people are the organization. They will no longer put up with working overtime just to get ahead in the office. It was like a 'badge of honor' to say how busy you were. It still is, but now, people are choosing differently. They are choosing to work in places where they feel valued and heard. People are not robots and if you treat them like robots then they will vote with their feet and leave.

This large turnover is costing organizations hand over fist. The leaders of these organizations are to blame. But the ultimate blame is with the organization's top leadership. If they are like some leaders I knew before the pandemic, who felt like it should be a privilege to work at their organization, then there will be a reckoning. No longer can leaders lead by title and command and control. People want more. They want to be engaged.

They want to be a part of the conversation. This is why leaders need to transform into a servant and transformational leader. A leader who inspires others to be their best. A leader who creates more leaders instead of followers. A leader who transforms the lives of others for good.

Like I said before, I had a transformation thrusted on me. I am so happy that it did. Without going through furlough, I wouldn't have had the courage to start my coaching business. To make matters worse, when I came back from the furlough, my job had been eliminated. That was the most crushing news of my life. I loved my job. At that time I didn't love my boss, but I loved what I did. I got to help people become the best leaders that they could be. I got to help others transform. Now, it was my turn.

I took a step out in faith and joined Powerful Women Today (PWT). The money to pay for it was a lot for me at the time but I knew I needed to join so that I could be with like-minded women and learn how to grow my skills and coaching business.

Even us strong women need help, support, and championing. That is what I got from PWT. I just kept at it. Even when things didn't seem like they would work out, I kept at it. It was my tenacity that helped me get through, but I wouldn't have had that if I didn't have PWT. It was the time that I invested in myself by taking the reins of my own life and doing the work that needed to be done to grow my business.

PWT took me out of my comfort zone and transformed me into the businesswoman that I am. If it wasn't for Carolina putting me on LinkedIn Live without any prep, I wouldn't be talking to a TV studio about becoming a host on one of their shows. I did a TV interview on coaching, and they thought that I did a great job with the interview and invited me to come back and host with them. How cool! I was able to do the interview without fear because I had done interviews with Carolina many times. This could be the start of yet another transformation in my career.

I never thought that I would be considered a bestselling author before becoming a bestselling speaker. Speaking is one of my true callings. Not in a bragging kind of way, but in a way to share a point. I have been mocked for my writing my whole life. It was bad. Like, really bad. Enough where my boss offered, no, demanded that I take a business writing course. Thankfully, I found a really good course. I wouldn't have ever, in a million years, thought that I would be a part of three best selling books and become a best selling author. Just because you aren't good at something doesn't mean that you can't learn or transform.

Transformation is a gift. Even if it is thrust upon you. So when you get that crappy feedback, the bad break, the loss of a job, the loss of a marriage, etc. Remember that you are not alone. Transformation is inevitable. We can embrace it, or it will embrace us.

I would like to invite you to start a journal as you embark on your transformation journey.

Week One:

Before you can transform, you first need to get clear on who you want to transform into. Who do you want to be? What is your WHY?

Each day this week, reflect on what brings you joy and fulfillment and write it down in your journal. Also reflect on the thing that takes joy away from you and write it down in your journal.

Week Two:

I'd like to invite you to review your lists from week one and answer the following questions.

- ❖ What is one small change that you can do to help you decrease the things that take away joy?
- ❖ What is one small change that will help you to add more joy to your life?
- ❖ Now, I challenge you to make these two small changes this week.

Week Three:

How did week two go? Were you able to make the two small changes?

- If yes, what helped you to stay accountable to your plan to change two small things in your life?
- What made the change possible?
- What system did you put in place to ensure accountability?
- If not, what can you do differently to ensure accountability towards your own goals?
- What made it challenging?
- How might you overcome that barrier?
- What perspective isn't serving you?

Week Four:

You are well on your way to transformation. Transformation happens in little steps made consistently over time. Repeat steps 1-3 until you've reached your goals of increasing joy and fulfillment and decreased the things that take your joy away.

If you'd like to dig deeper on your transformation, I'd love to coach you. Please feel free to reach out to mindy@mindycoaching.com to share your successes with the exercises, or if you'd like to try coaching. For those who buy this book, I am offering a free 30 minute transformation coaching session.

With gratitude,

Mindy McManus, MEd, PCC, SPC

Assistant Professor of Healthcare Administration at Mayo Clinic

ABOUT THE AUTHOR

My passion is to empower diverse individuals to unleash their leadership potential, improve decision-making, and reach their desired goals through an innovative coaching partnership to increase growth, satisfaction, success, and resiliency.

We partner together to harness the greatness within you and you'll learn how to lead yourself, others, and your organization/business. Women, in particular, tend to have self-limiting thoughts that keep them from reaching their full potential. That is where I come in to help defeat these thoughts and help my clients overcome the fear that holds them back.

What do I offer?

- » 1:1 and group coaching for individuals who want to set goals, change their lives, and take action towards the life they want.
- » Leadership development courses to help bridge the knowledge gap around leading self, others, and their organization/business.
- » Safe space to fight your inner-critic and create tactics to overcome the self-defeating thoughts from our inner-critic and imposter syndrome.
- » Organization Development (OD), Team development, Board retreats and Retreats

I am certified in the following Coaching arenas:

International Coaching Federation (ICF) Coach at the Professional Certified Coach (PCC) level

- » Certified Executive Coach, CEC
- » Certified Visionary Leadership Coach, CVLC

- » Certified Women Empowerment Coach
- » Certified MentorCoach, CMC
- » Crucial Conversations
- » Emotional Intelligence 2.0 and 360
- » Proci Change Management Practitioner
- » DiSC Instructor
- » Real Colors Facilitator

CONTACT INFORMATION

Mindy McMcManus
MINDY'S EXECUTIVE COACHING LLC
www.linkedin.com/in/mindygillis
mindy@mindycoaching.com
904-994-7023

Monika Greczek

Dedication

My Dedication it is to My Family, Friends, and Clients, for sharing your stories with me, which allows me to continue to do what's best for myself and you!

CHAPTER 12

HEALTHY HABITS

By Monika Greczek

Let me start by telling you that I did not know the habits that I created would impact my life. It wasn't until my adult life that I started reflecting on my past and noticed that change in my life and in myself. I wasn't comfortable in my body, and my mind was trying to tell me something. Except I kept saying, tomorrow I will start to work out, eat better, go to sleep earlier, finish my paperwork, meditate, read, pray, etc. Tomorrow turned into months, and those bad habits I created changed my mentality to negative things. I gained weight like never before, more than when I was pregnant with my son. I was procrastinating on paperwork, cleaning, not having enough energy to get through the day, tossing and turning when I tried to sleep, and the list goes on.

I realized that the habits I created only took me away from my goals, and the results were not what I expected. How could this happen? It happened and I needed to reflect on what I needed to do to create what I really wanted. I wasn't moving forward at all. Things were changing, but not for the good.

Healthy, Happy, and Positive Habits. How do I create this when I am constantly telling myself tomorrow, later, it isn't that bad, etc. I took a good look in the mirror and told myself to do it now before it's to late. You have everything you need. Now, one day, one breath, one meal, one step, one exercise, one positive thought, etc. You get what I am saying? Then repeat every day. That good habit will start producing results, changes, happiness, and whatever you heart desires.

> *"I took a good look in the mirror and told myself to do it now before it's to late"*

I started to go to the gym and put it my calendar, scheduled the classes, and made a commitment to myself that I will work out and get stronger each time. The first class was so hard, I had to take breaks and drink tons of water. I felt like I was going to faint. I couldn't get enough oxygen and my heart was beating so fast. I knew it was going to be challenging and that it would get better with time. I remembered 18 years ago when I was working out constantly, my body and my health got better. A year later and I am down 30 pounds, my BMI is no longer in the Obese category, it is at 24% which is incredible. I feel better because I am fueling my body with nutrient food, I sleep better because I made a habit of taking CBD every evening before I go to bed. Let me tell you, I sleep like a baby and wake up ready to start the day!

These good habits I created for myself canceled out the negative habits I had and started producing results. I realized that the first step wasn't as hard as I was putting into my mind. It's just like a when we ride a bike, we want to keep riding until we ride without our hands steering the handlebars, going as fast as you can without fear because you got this. Once you start doing something you choose to do, it becomes a habit and then produces results. When it becomes a good habit then it is easy to do, and you will enjoy doing it.

I love how I feal after I eat. No more bloating, food coma, and now I have the energy to do whatever I choose. I created a sleeping habit and look forward to going to bed because I am going to get a good nights' sleep. Paperwork gets done, as does cleaning, cooking, and everything else that I put on my list to accomplish. I am happier, healthier, and enthusiastic.

What good habits are you going to create? Remember, you will see the results if you choose to keep going and doing. Nothing happens in an instant. I don't know if you've ever had instant potatoes, they are not as good as real mashed potatoes. It takes time and when you reach your goal and dreams through the creation of those habits. Celebrate! You did it!!! One step, one breath, one goal, one healthy meal, etc. and you'll see what you can accomplish.

Just as the book is called 30 days to Transformation, it takes 30 days to create a Habit, keep up the good habit and celebrate your accomplishments!

ABOUT THE AUTHOR

Monika Greczek is a woman who has gone out and achieved her goals and continues to. She had started to envision the life she wanted to create since she was a young girl. Through all the books, coaching, classes, education, work, and intentions, she has followed her dreams. She started doing hair at the age of 14, won 1st place in the manikin competition at the Cosmetology school she attended, then went onto achieving all her goals and graduating top of her class. She received her Cosmetology License at 16 years of age and also was promoted at the salon to assistant manager. Doing hair came naturally to her. Her clients loved the way they looked and felt after receiving services from Monika, even now her clients love that they always feel better after their visit with her. She listens to herself and her clients and always does what is best. There are people from all over that come to see Monika and receive that magic though she has through doing hair, massage, body work, coaching and engaging with them. She has become a fabulous hair artist, mentor, and coach.

CONTACT INFORMATION

Monika Greczek
Email: extasyhair@comcast.net
Website: Naturahempco.com
LinkedIn: https://www.linkedin.com/in/monika-greczek-3710b225/

I am like a drop of water on a rock. After drip, drip, dripping in the same place, I begin to leave a mark, and I leave my mark in many people's hearts.
Rigoberta Menchu

Sallie Wagner

Dedication

I dedicate my chapter, TRANSFORMATION: YOUR STRATEGY FOR LIFE, to my children and grandchildren. May you be transformed by the renewing of your minds!

CHAPTER 13

TRANSFORMATION: YOUR STRATEGY FOR LIFE

By Sallie Wagner

For many years, I lived my life on the periphery. Skating around the edges. Paddling along in the shallow end of the pool of life. Because, while I was "enlightened" on the inside, I believed that that mindset, alone, was enough. So, I never fully lived it on the outside.

Then, suddenly, everything changed. And by suddenly, I mean gradually over many years. But my subjective experience was that it happened suddenly. So… suddenly… something in my thinking changed. I was transformed. I finally understood that if I truly believe what I claim I believe about myself and the nature of reality, then I **must** change my life to reflect and live out that belief in all areas of life – body, mind, spirit. So, I began to manifest that transformation externally in my life, in the landscape of my reality.

Admittedly, I took the scenic route to transformation. Now, I know that there are more direct ways to get there. And while it's all about the journey, we can all appreciate a few short cuts along the way. So, I'm sharing with you 3 key concepts that will accelerate you on your path to transformation in all areas of **your** life. Those 3 interconnected concepts are:

- ❖ Develop an overall strategy for your life
- ❖ Develop goals that support your strategy
- ❖ Develop systems and processes that support your goals

So, are you ready for transformation? Are you ready to accelerate that transformation? Then read on!

Transformation begins on the inside and is then manifested in the landscape of your reality

As I mentioned earlier, my transformation started with internal awareness. It started on the inside, and then I manifested it in the landscape of my reality. It all started with a decision. Everything begins with a decision. Not just wanting, but actually deciding. When you decide, the thing you've decided for happens.

As you make that decision in your life, you transform your thoughts and beliefs about yourself. Those thoughts and beliefs determine your feelings, which are transformed by those transformed thoughts and beliefs. Those feelings determine your decisions, which are also transformed by those transformed feelings. Those decisions determine your actions, which are likewise transformed by those transformed decisions. And those actions determine your results, which are now your choice, consistent with your transformed thoughts, feelings, decisions, and actions.

So, by design and natural progression, the internal transformation is manifested in the landscape of your reality through your decisions, actions, and results.

Now that you understand the progression, you're ready for the first step in your transformation – your overall strategy for your life.

Begin your transformation with an overall life strategy

The first manifestation of your decision to transform is to craft an overall life strategy, the overarching principle of your life, your raison d'etre.

This strategy is far bigger than a goal. Be sure you recognize the difference. For example, a strategy may be to be physically fit. A goal is to lose 10 pounds.

To formulate your strategy, begin by asking yourself questions. Who are your heroes? In literature, history, movies, mythology. These are people who make you think that you could do anything if you were like them. They reflect strengths that you value and aspire to. And the truth is, you already have those strengths in yourself.

Consider those strengths and how they empower those heroes in their approach to life. Are they courageous, clever, brave, strong, intelligent, wise, loving?

Chose 5-7 people – they are now your Transformation Advisory Board. Compile all their strengths into an overall approach to life, which now becomes **your** overall approach to life, your strategy. Express your strategy as your hero's mission in life – remember, you are the hero of your own story! Describe what you do, why you do it and who you do it for or to. Be as specific as possible, while also maintaining a universal application.

For example:

I build physical, emotional, mental, social resilience in life every day in order to live a long, prosperous, productive life, which empowers me to contribute my highest and best energies to my family, my community, and all of being.

Now that you have your heroic life strategy, you're ready to build goals that support it.

Support your life strategy with big, specific goals

Your next hero quest is to develop goals to support your life strategy. Your quest is to develop goals in each of the various areas of your life so that you can fully support your overall life strategy. By the way, these areas should also be part of your strategy, so review your strategy and make sure everything is included.

Those areas are:

- health and well-being
- relationships
- career/vocation
- recreation and free time
- personal
- finances
- contribution to the world

Here are three key guidelines for developing your goals. Certainly, you can use additional guidelines, just make sure you include these three:

- ❖ Make it big
- ❖ Ask the right questions
- ❖ Be specific

First, your goals should be big enough to support your heroic strategy. They should be so big that they scare you. They should be so big that people laugh when you tell them. If you're not scared, and people aren't laughing, your goals may not be big enough!

Next, ask the right questions. The quality of your life is determined by the quality of the questions you're willing to ask. So, ask the hard questions. Remember, you're the hero of your own story. So, ask heroic questions.

For example, why is a particular thing important to you? Is it important because you deem it to be worthy of your heroic quest? Or is it because somebody told you it **should** be important.

Last, you must be as specific as possible in stating your goals – if you don't specify, the universe will fill in the blanks and you may not get the results you intend. Remember, words matter. We've all heard the joke about the guy who wishes for a million bucks and suddenly he's surrounded by deer. Don't be like that guy!

Now that you have your heroic goals that support your heroic life strategy, you're ready to build the systems and processes that will ensure that you achieve those goals.

Support your goals with systems and processes for daily activities to move you in the right direction every day

As important as goals are, they're not enough. You need systems and processes that will support your daily efforts to achieve those goals. So, here's the 1st step in your system to launch into action:

Write your goals down

When you write down your goals, you increase your chances of success to 56%. It's so simple and so obvious people think it can't possibly make a difference! And yet it does.

The 2nd step in your system to launch into action:

Share your goals with somebody

Share your goals with family, friends, a goal buddy. SOMEBODY. And take the additional step of identifying specific action steps to take toward your goals, and you increase your chances of success to 64%.

Those action steps, that system and structure, are crucial. Because you see . . . goals alone won't get you there.

Instead of focusing exclusively on your goals – as wonderful and heroic as they are – create a reliable system, something that you can easily and readily and willingly repeat every day. That's goal setting to the present. Then, you succeed every day, not by reaching the goal, but by moving in the right direction. Every day.

And you're already 64% of the way there!

The 3rd step in your system is to launch into action:

Make weekly progress reports to that goal buddy

This is the accountability factor. When you do that, you increase your chances of success to 76%.

Now that you have your systems and processes in place, the next piece is to recognize your accomplishment. What you've done and continue to do is far beyond adopting a strategy, developing goals, and implementing systems and processes. You have reclaimed your power over your own transformation. Rather than leaving it to chance, happenstance, or unconscious programming from your paradigms, you have reclaimed conscious control over your own life.

When you reclaim your power over your own transformation, transformation itself becomes your life strategy

Interestingly, when you reclaim your power over your own transformation, transformation

becomes your life strategy. Because as you adopt a strategy using all of these guidelines, you have, in essence, adopted a strategy for transformation. The transformation is in the process, in the journey, not merely the destination.

And as you wield the power of your own transformation, you transform the world! What an amazingly powerful life strategy!

5 reflections for transformation as ***your*** life strategy

- ❖ Transformation begins on the inside and is then manifested in the landscape of your reality
- ❖ Begin your transformation with an overall life strategy
- ❖ Support your life strategy with big, specific goals
- ❖ Support your goals with systems and processes for daily activities to move you in the right direction every day
- ❖ When you reclaim your power over your own transformation, transformation itself becomes your life strategy

ABOUT THE AUTHOR

Sallie Wagner, Your Life Alchemist

Sallie specializes in helping women reclaim their power over their own lives. She uses Emotional Freedom Techniques (EFT), Evolved Neurolinguistic Programming (eNLP), and trauma-aware modalities so clients launch into action and gain access to rapid, concrete results as they ditch habits, behaviors, fears, phobias, limiting beliefs and decisions that hold them back in life.

Speaker, author, lawyer, real estate broker and instructor, and life coach, Sallie spent the majority of her law career in the corporate world, working in real estate for various industries. She currently owns and operates a company that provides broker and contract compliance services to real estate brokerages throughout Florida. Serving over 2,500 real estate agents, averaging 600 transactions each week, with annual sales volume in excess of $6 Billion, Sallie provides timely assistance to agents on contract questions and transaction pitfalls, facilitating as tens of thousands of families achieve their home ownership dreams.

Sallie also owns and operates a real estate school, providing exceptional educational opportunities for real estate professionals throughout Florida.

CONTACT INFORMATION

Sallie Wagner
Intentional Life Coaching LLC
swagner@salliewagnerenterprises.com
816.616.5403

Simone Sloan

Dedication

To servant leaders who put their teams' needs first and who help people to develop and to perform at their highest.

CHAPTER 14

TRANSFORMING TOXIC ROCKSTARS INTO SERVANT LEADERS

By Simone Sloan

Companies often have key employees with exceptional skills or knowledge that make them invaluable to a company's bottom line. But sometimes, these same people are terrible leaders who are harmful to those working with them. Invaluable yet noxious leaders are "toxic rockstars." That toxicity comes in all forms, shapes, and colours, and is harmful to the organization in both the short and long term, often driving away other talented individuals. As shown in a survey conducted by Payscale(1), employee turnover can lower employee morale, decrease productivity, and impact an organization's costs for recruiting, onboarding, and training.

Yes, they are "killin' it." But they are also killing their team in the process.

What do companies do with leaders who are too valuable to let go and too toxic to promote? I have worked with a lot of toxic rockstars, and I have found ways to transform even the most toxic rockstar into a thoughtful servant leader.

The primary traits of toxic rockstars

Toxic rockstars are not all toxic in the same way, but they have some commonalities. Most notably, it is always all about them.

Toxic rockstars have an "I and I alone" mentality. I and I alone know what I am doing. I and I alone can handle this. They never look to their team for ideas. In meetings, they do all of the talking. They have no interest in mentoring anyone because their only concern is advancing themselves.

In a company, most people know who the toxic rockstars are and their enablers. The exception is the toxic rockstars themselves, who lack the self-awareness to understand the unintended impact of their conduct. They have no idea that people feel damaged by their actions, communications, and behaviors. They do not see the resentment from their team. They live in a bubble and as a result, think that they are doing a great job all around and that everyone agrees with their performance and leadership style.

Toxic rockstars are often successful because they are focused on the specific tasks that let them produce. However, they do not have a vision for their leadership. They do not even have a vision for their life outside of work. They have never considered the questions, "who am I, and am I living my best life?"

Toxic Rockstar Types

In my work, I have identified three predominant toxic rockstar management pathologies.

Command and Conquer

Combative, transactional, and self-serving, the command and conquer leader sees their team as opponents.

Mistrustful of Others

These are the leaders who think of their teams as a bunch of idiots and slackers who could never do what they do. They want to make sure everyone knows that without them everything would fall apart.

Mistrustful of Self

These leaders are unable to make decisions and are afraid to share ideas for fear of being ridiculed. They focus on keeping their heads down and trying to be invisible. They do not see themselves as toxic rockstars, but as leaders striving to be perfectionists.

> Transforming a toxic rockstar into a servant leader takes time, but it can be done.

To show you how it is done, let me tell you about three rockstars that I detoxified.

Robert (Command and Conquer)

Robert's team did not really trust nor liked him. They suspected him of having a secret agenda for getting ahead, and were frustrated by his volatile temper and erratic actions.

Still, Robert consistently produced great results. In most ways, he was a great candidate for promotion. But the company feared that his bad leadership behaviours would make him a greater liability in a higher position.

I had twelve virtual sessions with Robert over six months.

He did not take the process seriously at first, coming to meetings unprepared and refusing to turn his camera on. To gain his trust, I offered him confidentiality and refused to judge him. *When he would rant about his team, or the company, or my process, instead of reacting in kind I would ask him, "what do you need?"* The question caught him by surprise. He said no one ever asked him what he needed.

We did mindfulness exercises and worked on deep breathing as a method to control his emotions.

The big breakthrough was when Robert had to have a 30-minute meeting with each team member in which he was only allowed to listen. Robert usually did all the talking in meetings, and he was shocked to learn how much pain he was causing. He had believed that everyone loved him.

He later sought out feedback from people outside of work and discovered that they had similar complaints. He realized that he was the only person he knew who did not see his toxicity.

Robert went from resenting our sessions to actively participating in them. He asked questions and even turned on his camera. He took up meditation, started practicing gratitude, and began acknowledging his team's efforts.

I kept the stakeholders of this process in the loop, and in turn, they let me know that they were observing changes. These changes in Robert did not appear to be performative, but were part of a genuine transformation.

Shana (Mistrustful of Others)

Shana did not trust anyone on her team and hated to delegate anything. She kept doing other people's work for them, making it clear how little faith she had in them. She resented the extra work she chose to do, but was eager to get all the credit for any successes of her team.

Shana had a specific knowledge set that made her invaluable to the company. Her management style was fairly typical of those who had once managed her. Unbeknownst to her, the company culture had changed, and newer employees were deeply dissatisfied with her leadership style.

In our sessions, Shana made it clear that she did not need any help and that what she was doing was working just fine. Like Robert, she would not turn on her camera.

Her main concern was what I would tell management, who wanted regular progress reports. I told her exactly what she needed to do to succeed in the process. I advised her how committing to the work could paint a powerful picture of improvement to change management's hearts and minds.

Once again, feedback from her team was a revelation to her. *Her big breakthrough was from reading about armored leaders and daring leaders in Brene Brown's Dare to Lead.* She realized that her armored leadership style was working against her.

On her next project, Shana decided to listen while letting her team drive. She stayed in an advisory role, learning to delegate while they ran the project. Soon after that, she was promoted.

Joan (Mistrustful of Self)

Joan was risk averse. Her fear of being blamed for mistakes led her to micromanage her team and delay making decisions. This damaged her team, who were unclear on direction and felt undermined by her constant second-guessing of herself. Her myopic focus helped neither the team nor the wider company. Feeling that she was barely holding on, her entire life had become just waking up, working all day, going home and feeding her kids, and doing it again the next day.

While Joan was effective in her current role and position, management needed her team to grow and was concerned that adding more people would magnify her leadership deficits.

Joan was uncomfortable during our sessions, afraid of anything that might feel like criticism. The company culture had never been defined because the company was built from a series of mergers. Her own managers had never given her helpful feedback, so she had never learned how to give it.

I worked with Joan on both inner and outer confidence. She worked on her body position, learning how to stand with pride and confidence. Before we worked together, Joan had never taken the time to celebrate her wins or those of her team, instead focusing on what she had not achieved or still had to do. So together we spent a few minutes of each session celebrating every win, no matter how small, and talking enthusiastically about her latest achievements.

I gathered team feedback and Joan teared up as she read it, finally understanding how her team saw her. This helped her understand the value in opening herself up to uncomfortable learning.

By the end of our sessions, Joan had agreed to let go and delegate more in areas we had identified, created work boundaries so she could think out problems without distractions, and instituted Steven Covey's time management system. Joan could finally breathe, and her team relaxed with her.

How to deal with your toxic rockstars – and prevent future ones

The tools I use to transform toxic leaders can also be used to mitigate the emergence of toxic tendencies. Poor leadership styles can be learned from other poor leaders or companies that do not intentionally nurture and invest in their cultures.

As shown in the McKinsey 2020 report, Diversity Wins: How Inclusion Matters (2), strengthening leaders' accountability and capability for inclusion is crucial for creating a better corporate culture, as is upholding a zero-tolerance policy for bullying, harassment, and microaggressions. There are many systemic changes that can make a company more resistant to toxic rockstar issues:

Create a safe environment to give and receive feedback. Creating a safe feedback loop was incredibly effective in each of these situations. Anonymous 360 reviews work well for this.

Create a culture that is inclusive of everyone. All leaders design and create an environment that can drive the high-performance behaviours needed to foster inclusion. Creating this inclusive work environment takes time. It requires much work and effort to intentionally foster a culture that is mindful of communication across teams and models consistency and commitment to company values.

Emphasize accountability and instill trust, care, and diversity. Culture is simply how things are done between people. Just replacing micro-aggressions with micro-inclusions as simple as smiles and eye contact can help people feel accepted and included. Companies should also ensure that leadership receives inclusivity training that gives them tools to address these issues and a safe space to practice new behaviours.

A company should not be hesitant to try and change its toxic rockstars in a way that lets them *keep their great qualities but change how they relate to others*. This investment in the people demonstrates a commitment to improving and evolving the company's culture. A Deloitte Global 2022 Gen Z and Millennial Survey (3) stated that 40% of respondents who identified as Gen Z and millennials stated that they rejected a job or assignment because it did not align with their values.

Transforming a toxic rockstar requires changes in both mindset and behaviour. *A leader who can replace assumptions with curiosity and judgments with an open, listening attitude is well on the way to shedding their toxicity.* Cameron and Seppala, in *The Best Leaders Have a Contagious Positive Energy (4)*, mention positive energizers. These are leaders who uplift others and themselves through authentic, values-based leadership. The impact of these behaviours has a positive impact on the organization in areas such as innovation, teamwork, financial performance, and workplace cohesion. When rockstars change their focus from themselves to strengthening and mentoring their teams, the value they bring to a company increases dramatically.

REFERENCES

(1) Payscale, Are You At Increased Risk For Employee Turnover In 2022?

(2) McKinsey & Company, Diversity Wins: How Inclusion Matters, 2020

(3) Deloitte, Striving for Balance, Advocating for Change, 2022

(4) Seppälä, Cameron in the Harvard Business Review, April, 2022

ABOUT THE AUTHOR

Simone Sloan is the founder of Your Choice Coach, an executive coaching and diversity, equity, and inclusion consulting firm.

CONTACT INFORMATION

To learn more, visit www.YourChoiceCoach.com or Email: info@yourchoicecoach.com

"Don't think about making women fit the world — think about making the world fit women."
Gloria Steinem

Youssef Skalli

Dedication

In memory of my grandmother, who encouraged me to embrace change with open mind, heart and arms.

CHAPTER 15

A TRANSFORMATION JOURNEY TOWARDS CULTURAL HUMILITY

By Youssef Skalli

"What is here is elsewhere, what is not here is nowhere" said to me my grandmother, "Lalla" as I loved to call her, with a shaken voice while gently laying her hand over my heart before hugging me strongly... I can still sense the smell of her rose scented perfume.

On that very warm 24th of August afternoon, I had just finished packing my suitcases to move abroad for what would be the first of many serial international assignments.

Family and friends gathered to bid me farewell, and each one had a piece of advice on a cultural aspect of my soon to be host country which, at that time, only my parents and Lalla had visited.

Of course, our neighbor Mr. Kia was there too; it is not his real name but let's stick to Kia, as that's what Lalla and I used to call him, for it stood for Know-It-All.

Just before leaving, Mr. Kia insisted kindly to give me a 15-minute lecture on my destination, a set of do's and don'ts, how people supposedly behave there, what might make them happy and what might upset them. You may have a Kia person in your social circle and can imagine how the conversation goes.

Back to Lalla, that sentence that concluded my conversation with her, became my happy compass wherever I go. In that same conversation, Lalla told me "Your heart is a big sponge, keep it open to absorb what comes its way and remember to squeeze it from time to time to make it lighter when needed and make room to absorb more".

Fast forward twenty years, I settled in Canada after having lived and worked in different countries, more precisely I had been based in 7 countries, had work assignments in 15, visited 37 and interacted with people from various backgrounds and over 60 nationalities, and still counting…

Before each assignment, business trip or leisure travel, I used to spend hours researching about my destination country. For my long-term assignments, I would attend a cultural orientation training designed for expatriates to ease our integration into the host country.

I am intentionally not naming any country here, I leave the door open to your imagination to take you wherever you feel like, because my lived experiences, and most probably yours too, are not about any specific country as much as about intercultural human interactions.

As per some professional standards, by now I would qualify for a "Cultural Competency" badge.

What does it mean to be culturally competent? Does it require you to travel the world to develop a cultural competence or competency? Can you really become a cultural competence expert?

Spoiler alert! Over the years I came to the conclusion that while I continue developing a sense of cultural curiosity, I am not, and cannot be, culturally competent, and I do not think you can be either.

I invite you to pause here for a moment and think first of what your definition of the term "culture" is, what do you think it is? And later, ask others around you to share their definition of culture.

I have been doing this exercise for years, and every time I am amazed by the different answers I get from myself and from others.

The words that come often are race, ethnicity, customs, shared beliefs, transferred knowledge, common social behaviors, manners, etiquette, food, art, learned traditions, transmitted values... The list keeps growing every time.

I did not have the chance to ask Mr. Kia, but maybe like me, you will be surprised that there is no commonly agreed upon definition of the word "culture" even though it is one of the most used words universally.

Cambridge dictionary, however, defines culture as "The way of life, especially the general customs and beliefs, of a particular group of people at a particular time". I like the fact that this definition includes a time dimension which makes it a living and evolving concept. Yet it has the limitation of eliminating any individuality aspect and presumes that every person adheres to all cultural customs and beliefs of the group they seem to belong to, and that one person can belong only to one specific group at a time excluding any possible intersectionality.

Think of your own family members. While there might be some common traits, values, habits, or rituals you share, would you consider that your life experiences are all identical? Don't you see that you have differences as well? That each member of the family has something unique about themselves that makes them have different opinions, beliefs, or abilities?

> *"I am ignorant of absolute truth. But I am humble before my ignorance and therein lies my honor and my reward."*
> – Gibran Khalil Gibran

Thinking back on the different cultural orientation or cultural competency trainings I attended, while it provided me at the time with basic knowledge about geography, history, verbal and nonverbal language hints, commonly accepted social courtesy and manners practiced in my destination, it was also unintentionally injecting my brain with some stereotypes and nurturing some of my implicit biases.

In a country where I was told that it is inappropriate to have eye contact with women, the first time my neighbor Fadi invited me for dinner at their place, I got ridiculed; first because my lack of eye contact was interpreted as a lack of respect towards Rania, his wife, and second because I complimented Rania on how delicious the soup was that Fadi actually prepared. Mr. Kia got it all wrong and so I did. Likely, Fadi and Rania were aware of the stereotypes associated with their country and they were open to share their interpretation of my behavior, giving me the opportunity to try explaining the context behind it. We have since become friends and still laugh about that evening.

I could write a complete book about similar situations where my supposed cultural competence turned into a cultural incompetence towards individuals. Those experiences developed in me a sense of humility and further curiosity.

Cherishing the advice of Lalla, I carry with me in my heart everywhere those lived experiences that made me realize that cultural awareness, sensitivity, competence, and curiosity are a life-long learning and unlearning process, a continuous exchange of knowledge between humans with no end-result other than appreciating the journey and the growth mindset it cultivates. I make sure to squeeze regularly so that I dispose of unhelpful biases and make room for new learnings.

When it comes to cultural identity, it is very common to rely on generalization and associate individuals with a predefined set of attributes. Being self-aware of this cognitive distortion leads to an enriching perspective in human relationships and understanding that cultural identity is a multidimensional concept.

The first time I took a global leadership position, I made sure to reflect first on what I think is my own cultural identity and asked each team member to do the same. Then we did a group exercise where each one of us shared what we thought were the main traits and values of other members. The reductive result was an eye opener to each one of us, as while we focused on one dimension, up to three in the best case, most of us on race, country, and visible gender, we missed many other dimensions.

That simple yet effective exercise allowed us to set the grounding foundations of our efficiently inclusive collaboration afterwards, where the uniqueness of each member was appreciated and celebrated. Tempted by the common trends, I felt the need to come out with a name for that exercise, first I called it "cultural fluidity," until one day I was having a conversation with my friend Eva, a medical doctor, and she mentioned the expression "Cultural Humility" which I found very interesting. Eva pointed me towards an article published in 1998 by MDs Melanie Tervalon and Jann Murray Garcia to whom the term cultural humility was first attributed. I became interested to know more about it and found out that it was a term gaining a certain popularity within the healthcare profession as a conceptual framework guiding the physician-patient dynamic.

The work of professors Tervalon and Garcia was fully aligned with my lived experiences and provided me with the term "cultural humility," which I immediately realized the benefit of its use as a relational leadership practice beyond the healthcare field. I then started coining it in my interactions with my colleagues and team members and it became an integrated part of my overall social behavior.

> *"The good life is a process, not a state of being. It is a direction not a destination."*
> *– Carl Rogers*

Approaching people from a stand of cultural humility involves a harmony with oneself. It is a continuous practice of congruence in one's life. For me, it opened an ocean of opportunities in my leadership roles, in my coaching practice, and in my interpersonal relations.

This self-awareness along with the genuine curiosity and practice of cultural humility in my interactions with others also highlighted an aspect of cultural identity that I used to disregard, which is the money mindset and how the culture impacts personal finances decisions.

Like other pillars of our cultural identity, I understood that each one of us has a personal tale that we build up over the years about personal finances. A tale instilled by our backgrounds and experiences. We end up cultivating a set of money-emotions that unconsciously influence our financial decisions and how we use money in our daily life.

In his bestselling book "the psychology of money: Timeless lessons on wealth, greed and happiness", Morgan Housel describes that better by stating: "every financial decision a person makes, makes sense to them in that moment and checks the boxes they need to check. They tell themselves a story about what they're doing and why they're doing it, and that story has been shaped by their own unique experiences."

The good news is that our experiences compile and keep teaching us new lessons. Therefore, we can write new chapters in our money tale. The same applies to others who come from various backgrounds and have distinct histories which made them develop a different relationship with money. We tend to tag people with labels based on the visible part of their financial behavior the same way we do with other constituents of perceived cultural dimensions.

A multitude of academic research and studies tried to tie money to happiness, two abstract and subjective concepts. No wonder the conclusion varies depending on the size and diversity of the population sample studied, and while some reached an indirect correlation, most agree with an Albert Einstein quote "not everything that can be counted counts, and not everything that counts can be counted."

Looking at that from the lens of cultural humility allows you to better understand that your definition of happiness and of money are unique to you, and so they are to every person.

Understanding the story you tell yourself about money, opening up to others' stories, and recognizing the differences gives you the opportunity to rewrite it if necessary and helping others to do the same if they need your help and ask for it.

Whether in my personal interactions or in my professional ones during my corporate career, both in finance and human resources, or now in my coaching practice, I rely on the cultural humility mindset, especially the self-reflection and lifelong learning, to continue breaking barriers and building bridges.

Whenever I am in a new environment and asked what brought me that far, I consistently answer that my F.A.R.s, Feelings, Actions and Results, took me far. I invite you to allow your thoughts to activate your F.A.R.s and enjoy the journey.

Unleash the drive to try new things, maintain a culture of transformation while staying true to your values and you will see a long-lasting change in multiple areas of your life.

> *"Do the best you can until you know better. Then when you know better, do better."*
> *– Maya Angelou*

ABOUT THE AUTHOR

Youssef Skalli is an enthusiastic professional globetrotter with 20+ years of progressive experience in a multinational corporate world.

After a successful career in Finance, driven by his passion for people development and empowerment, talent management, coaching and mentoring, organization effectiveness, multi-dimensional diversity and inclusion, along with strong appreciation of human capital value, Youssef landed in HR to lead different transformational projects aligning HR initiatives with business vision and strategic goals.

Having proved himself in corporate life in different countries and multicultural contexts across the 3 continents of Africa, Asia and Europe, he moved recently to North America and settled in Ottawa, Canada.

Youssef sees in this new settlement an opportunity to carry on with his lifelong learning journey and self-development. He tends to be an adventurer who seizes every chance to fulfill his motto: "Do more of what makes you happy, here and now!"

He embraces the new context through a rich panel of activities and hobbies such as, mental health advocacy, volunteering, reading, writing, creative cooking, interior remodeling, short family videos creation and singing… terribly!

CONTACT INFORMATION

Youssef Skalli
SKALLIbility Coaching
Website: skallibility.com
Email: Youssef@skallibility.com
LinkedIn: https://www.linkedin.com/in/MySkalli

"Sometimes you have to let everything go – purge yourself. If you are unhappy with anything – whatever is bringing you down – get rid of it. Because you will find that when you are free, your true creativity, your true self comes out."
~ Tina Turner

CONCLUSION

How to become a subject matter expert by Melanie Herschorn

Transforming into the expert you want to be is less not about spending the 10,000 hours to hone your craft, a number that's been attributed to author Malcolm Gladwell. You don't even have to be a "professional" (whatever the heck that means).

What you really need to have is the right mindset and a few tools in your arsenal that I've outlined below.

Yes. It can be that uncomplicated. It can even be done without attending medical school.

I know lots a lot of experts who are too encumbered by imposter syndrome to charge for their expertise. I used to be (and sometimes still am) one of them. Even my dog sitter has trouble asking for her desired fee after 28 years in the business.

Feelings Matter

The "feeling" part is important to touch upon. Many of us are our own worst enemies. We can get all the positive feedback in the world but if we hear one negative comment, we'll fixate on it. If one person says something that triggers us to make us question our expertise, we're likely to wonder if we should just throw in the towel now.

Whenever this happens, I want you to go back to tools 1 through 3. Read something to make you feel like you've gained some new knowledge. Share that knowledge with someone you can help. Then, consider writing about your expertise in a book so that you can support even more people across the globe. With a book and a plan to market it, the sky is the limit.

Tapping Into the Power of Transformation: Turning your Mess into Your Message by Mindy McManus

I never thought that I would be considered a bestselling author before becoming a bestselling speaker. Speaking is one of my true callings. Not in a bragging kind of way, but in a way to share a point. I have been mocked for my writing my whole life. It was bad. Like, really bad. Enough where my boss offered, no, demanded that I take a business writing course. Thankfully, I found a really good course. I wouldn't have ever, in a million years, thought that I would be a part of three best selling books and become a best selling author. Just because you aren't good at something doesn't mean that you can't learn or transform.

Transformation is a gift. Even if it is thrust upon you. So when you get that crappy feedback, the bad break, the loss of a job, the loss of a marriage, etc. Remember that you are not alone. Transformation is inevitable. We can embrace it, or it will embrace us.

I would like to invite you to start a journal as you embark on your transformation journey.

Healthy Habits by Monika Greczek

I realized that the habits I created only took me away from my goals, and the results were not what I expected. How could this happen? It happened and I needed to reflect on what I needed to do to create what I really wanted. I wasn't moving forward at all. Things were changing, but not for the good.

Healthy, Happy, and Positive Habits. How do I create this when I am constantly telling myself tomorrow, later, it isn't that bad, etc. I took a good look in the mirror and told myself to do it now before it's to late. You have everything you need. Now, one day, one breathe, one meal, one step, one exercise, one positive thought, etc. You get what I am saying? Then repeat every day. That good habit will start producing results, changes, happiness, and whatever you heart desires.

Transformation: Your Strategy for Life by Sallie Wagner

*Transformation begins on the inside
and is then manifested in the
landscape of your reality*

As I mentioned earlier, my transformation started with internal awareness. It started on the inside, and then I manifested it in the landscape of my reality. It all started with a decision. Everything begins with a decision. Not just wanting, but actually deciding. When you decide, the thing you've decided for happens.

As you make that decision in your life, you transform your thoughts and beliefs about yourself. Those thoughts and beliefs determine your feelings, which are transformed by those transformed thoughts and beliefs. Those feelings determine your decisions, which are also transformed by those transformed feelings. Those decisions determine your actions, which are likewise transformed by those transformed decisions. And those actions determine your results, which are now your choice, consistent with your transformed thoughts, feelings, decisions, and actions.

So, by design and natural progression, the internal transformation is manifested in the landscape of your reality through your decisions, actions, and results.

Now that you understand the progression, you're ready for the first step in your transformation – your overall strategy for your life.

TRANSFORMING YOUR LEADERSHIP AND IMPACT ON OTHERS

Transforming Toxic Rockstars into Servant Leaders by Simone Sloan

Toxic rockstars have an "I and I alone" mentality. I and I alone know what I am doing. I and I alone can handle this. They never look to their team for ideas. In meetings, they do all of the talking. They have no interest in mentoring anyone, because their only concern is advancing themselves.

In a company, most people know who the toxic rockstars are and their enablers. The exception is the toxic rockstars themselves, who lack the self-awareness to understand the unintended impact of their conduct. They have no idea that people feel damaged by their actions, communications, and behaviors. They do not see the resentment from their team. They live in a bubble and as a result, think that they are doing a great job all around and that everyone agrees with their performance and leadership style.

Toxic rockstars are often successful because they are focused on the specific tasks that let them produce. However, they do not have a vision for their leadership. They do not even have a vision for their life outside of work. They have never considered the questions, "who am I, and am I living my best life?"

A transformation journey towards cultural humility by Youssef Skalli

"What is here is elsewhere, what is not here is nowhere" said to me my grandmother, "Lalla" as I loved to call her, with a shaken voice while gently laying her hand over my heart before hugging me strongly... I can still sense the smell of her rose scented perfume.

As per some professional standards, by now I would qualify for a "Cultural Competency" badge.

What does it mean to be culturally competent? Does it require you to travel the world to develop a cultural competence or competency? Can you really become a cultural competence expert?

Spoiler alert! Over the years I came to the conclusion that while I continue developing a sense of cultural curiosity, I am not, and cannot be, culturally competent, and I do not think you can be either.

I invite you to pause here for a moment and think first of what is your definition of the term "culture" is, what do you think culture it is? And later, ask others around you to share their definition of culture.

Understanding the story you tell yourself about money, opening up to others' stories, and recognizing the differences gives you the opportunity to rewrite it if necessary and helping others to do the same if they need your help and ask for it.

Unleash the drive to try new things, maintain a culture of transformation while staying true to your values and you will see a long-lasting change in multiple areas of your life.

> *"Do the best you can until you know better. Then when you know better, do better."*
> *– Maya Angelou*

ACKNOWLEDGEMENTS

I often say that Powerful Women Today chose me instead of the other way around. Really, I believe the teachers, mentors, champions and critics of Powerful Women Today are also called to it. In the ten-plus years that we have championed and empowered women's emotional and financial independence, organic transformation has been the absolute foundation of our journey and our success. Never rigid, always allowing for growth, change and possibilities each person leaving a mark and it left its mark on each and every person. Second to my son, Powerful Women Today is the privilege of my life and the essence of what I hope is a legacy of inspiration for empowerment and possibilities.

Carolina M. Billings
Founder & CEO

SPECIAL THANKS TO

OUR PWT MENTOR EXPERTS

Their brilliance, generosity and thought leadership light the way to bring knowledge, hope and encouragement to women and men all over the world.

OUR PUBLISHING TEAM

Dortha Hise. Our layout and publishing architect. Her joining PWT enabled us to fully become our own PWT Publishing press bringing all elements of publication in-house. Thank you for your dedication and discipline.

Cristina Sciarra. Your editing and grammar help us present our words forward.

Stacey Hall, Our Book Launch Strategist champions our authors and audiences on launch day.

Melanie Herschorn, Our book promotion and book marketing expert helping us bring our message of hope to the world.

ABOUT POWERFUL WOMEN TODAY & PWT PUBLISHING

For an empowered woman, challenges are not a time for crisis, they are a time for action.
— Carolina M. Billings

POWERFUL WOMEN TODAY IS A GLOBAL COMMUNITY of Highly Influential Women Entrepreneurs and Professional Women Who Want to Make a Difference in The World by Showcasing Their Voice, Expertise, Talents, Experience and Passion

Empowerment is about taking action... No more apologies to anyone by any woman ever again when you embrace empowerment! Especially no apologies for being true to yourself and for going after what you want. Powerful Women are fierce defenders of joy, happiness and independence and honour themselves and their own decisions.

As women, we are often taught in society to be good girls, get good grades, get a job, get married, and have children. But luckily times have changed for women today — we now have the choice to be powerful and live life by our own set of rules. Powerful Women's greatest gifts are to trust their intuition and to learn to put themselves first so they can be the best unique version of themselves, and give back to the world — Unapologetically!

MISSION

To Champion and Empower Women's Emotional and Financial Independence.

VISION

To Champion Emotionally Independent women with literacy and maturity who have agency, and know how to negotiate win/win/win solutions that serve not only the world but self. She knows to have intelligent, productive and timely conversations that lead to desired outcomes. She knows that it is self-accountability not blaming others that leads to success.

A Financial Independent woman does not have to compromise her values, self-worth, and builds the life she deserves for herself and those she leads and serves. A woman with Financial Literacy has Emotional Maturity that leads to Freedom.

OUR CORE VALUES

We believe,
In Courage
In Character
In Supporting and Championing

In Resolution and Reconciliation

In Responsibility
In Action not Words

In Honouring Diversity and Active Inclusion

In Free Will and Self Agency

We believe,
That there is an opportunity for Greatness at Powerful Women Today

That We are #StrongerTogether
That Empowered Women must Empower Women
That There are no problems but opportunities for growth

That Our Differences are our Blessings that must be Honoured Respect above all else.
That Deeds Speak, Intentions Whisper
In Giving before Receiving.

OUR ECOSYSTEM

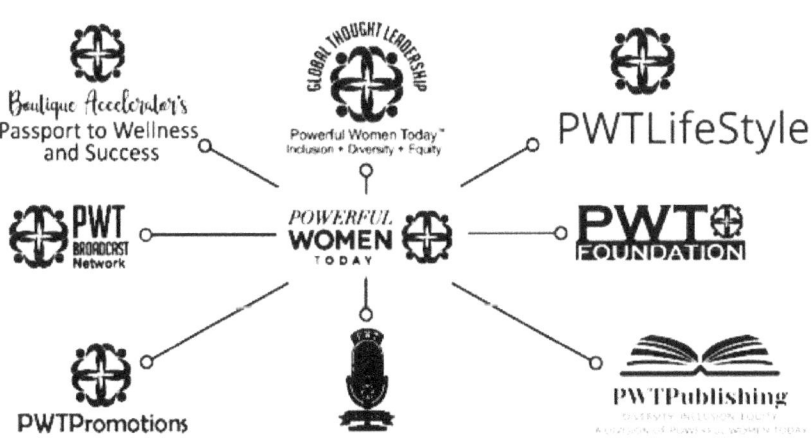

Visit our Website:
www.powerfulwomentoday.com

Contact us at:
Publisher@powerfulwomentoday.com

Join our Newsletter:
https://www.linkedin.com/newsletters/6861823529403465728/

Follow us on Social Media:

www.linkedin.com/in/carolinabillings/

www.youtube.com/channel/UCkI5hW2Z5Uz3daMxQFVRE_w

Join our LIVE Podcast Tuesdays at 7:00 PM EST via LinkedIn Audio

PWTPublishing
DIVERSITY INCLUSION EQUITY
A DIVISION OF POWERFUL WOMEN TODAY

Imagine

WHAT IF YOU HAD EVERYTHING YOU NEED TO PUBLISH A BESTSELLING BOOK ALL IN ONE PLACE?

Most people I meet all around the world have an ingrained belief that writing a book is an insurmountable task that is only for those with a literary degree, not a coach, consultant, practitioner, speaker, healer or entrepreneur... and up until recently, it was!

**DITCH YOUR FEARS, NOT YOUR DREAMS
WRITE YOUR BOOK NOW**

Why Publish a Book?

We believe it is the time in history for women to begin to document their journey and stories. **Throughout history, women have played a major role** in scientific discovery, literature and the arts **yet their names have been omitted or forgotten**.

PWTPublishing a division of Powerful Women Today is committed to **Diversity, Equity and Inclusion of all voices ready to share their gifts and thought leadership with the world**. We specialize primarily in removing barriers to entry for women authors and those who **champion women's advancement**, safety and progress. **Our multi-media publishing style maximizes the author's visibility and content distribution**. Are you ready to make history?

Multi Media Publishing

Our point of difference is that we provide a package that includes all the mentoring, content structure, editing, layout, publishing, Amazon Bestseller Campaign, upload and eBook, pre-launch, and marketing guidance. We also give group support in private, author-only groups.

TOP 5 REASONS TO PUBLISH

1. to Build a Brand & Grow Your Business
2. to Build a Legacy
3. for Thought Leadership
4. to Fundraise
5. publishing as Income

www.powerfulwomentoday.com

OTHER PWT PUBLISHING PUBLICATIONS

Purchase Now

Purchase Now

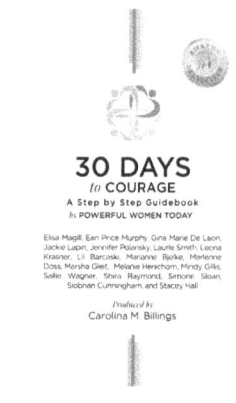

Purchase Now

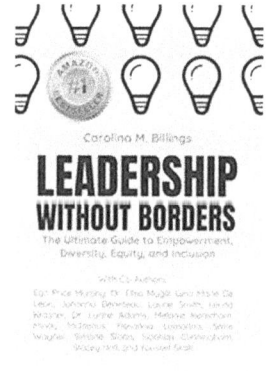

Purchase Now

Purchase Now

Available On Amazon and Anywhere Books Are Sold

> *"Her courage was her crown, and she wore it like a Queen."*
> *Atticus*

www.ingramcontent.com/pod-product-compliance
Lightning Source LLC
Chambersburg PA
CBHW041305110526
44590CB00028B/4247